Dear Hayley

TREVOR WRIGHT

ISBN: 978-0-9563948-2-8

DEDICATION

This book is dedicated to my wonderful grandchildren,
Jessica and Jasper, and
My constant feline companion, Paws.

CONTENTS

	Acknowledgments	7
	Friendship	9
	Preface	11
1	North Africa to Cowden	15
2	The First Encounter	26
3	The In-between Years	41
4	Renewed Beginnings	58
5	We Tie the Knot and Share Champers with Hayley	67
6	Work and Babies	73
7	Heartache	79
8	The Times Are a Changin'	113
9	Amazing Times	128
10	U.S.A to Africa to Australia	158
11	Four Legged Friends	170
12	Africa Revisited	184
13	The Last Word is Left to Hayley	197
	Epilogue	210
	Letters	212

ACKNOWLEDGMENTS

Thank you to my 'Little Big Sister' Carol Pankhurst for the cover artwork, especially the path extending into the far distance of time.

My gratitude to both Robin Moody and Dr. Claudia Garratt, for the endless hours of painstaking proofreading, pointing out wonderful 'schoolboy howlers', such as mentioning a fleet of Spitfires, opposed to a squadron of Spitfires!

A special thank you must be extended to my son Joe, who, despite a heavy work schedule, managed to find time to assemble this book, and take the project to print status.

FRIENDSHIP

If I were to dream, a dream,
Where greys and browns are forever banished,
And colours of such hue,
To raise even the dullest from their slumbers.
Then I would choose you,
Whose colours reflect the fragrance of a mind,
So full of gaiety, eyes full of wonder.

Trevor Wright

PREFACE

Many, many years ago, in the late seventies, while at a family wedding, a cousin confronted me, as she heard that I somehow befriended Hayley Mills, the famous Disney star. She made it abundantly clear that she did not believe the story whatsoever by saying, and I quote:

"People like her do not associate with people like you!" I found that a profoundly sad indictment of society. It is a far richer experience to chat and listen to all of society than to limit yourself on the basis of job status, size of your house or your bank balance! Having digested this notion, however, it then occurred to me that this particular person, when accused previously of being a snob, responded by indignantly protesting using this wonderful little gem: "A snob? I am certainly not a snob. I even talked to the milkman!"

Hayley said on one occasion that fame can be an illusion, and I tend to agree. After all, strip away the cloak of celebrity, and you have a human being who will experience all the same doubts, insecurities, the good times, the bad times, and the great leveller of all, the daily visit to the loo!

My story with Hayley must be fairly unique, in that it has lasted sixty years and all started by a moment in time. If I am honest, initially I was just one of millions of besotted teenage fans around the world who idolised her. Just the same as Hayley, in turn, as a teenager, had a crush on Elvis Presley! I guess a vast proportion of the population has been infatuated with some form of celebrity at some time in their life. In most cases, it fades into pleasant memories, with the possible exception of football, which not only has individual player adulation, but also team worship for life! Having dipped my toe into the many Hayley Mills global fan clubs, it is evident that she too has a vast army of people who have followed her for decades! From our first meeting, my adolescent teenage adulation of Hayley morphed into a lasting platonic friendship. This is a story of two entirely different lives, which have periodically crossed paths either by backstage chats or invites to her home, but always linked by continuing correspondence. Over the years, I believe I have amassed a collection of some one hundred and eighty letters, Christmas and other greeting cards written from various parts of the world. Lately, we tend to use emails which, apart from instant messaging, offer a bonus of no postage stamp into the bargain! Originally, this letter collection lived in my 'memories box' alongside items such as the last tram ticket issued in London or my old school report, which had followed my entire scholastic career in book form, and also, would you believe, even my old school tie! In addition, an early musician's union card, which was vital to perform in any class A venue, plus a rather crumpled set list from an early sixties gig. The memory box remains also home to my first driving licence issued in 1962! The letters from Hayley now reside in a very impressive stock book of their own.

Hayley is a remarkable person, having coped with international success at such a tender age and coping with the confines that come with it. Being a member of possibly one of the most famous renowned acting families, she would have rubbed shoulders with many well-known actors from both the theatre and the silver screen. To us on the outside, this would represent a fantastic lifestyle, which is true, but it did occur to me, there was probably a downside too. Not experiencing that crazy teenager time, taking off with your friends and doing stuff, or wearing clothes your parents might frown on! At roughly the same time as Hayley embarked on her first film, "Tiger Bay", I was rocking and rolling with Folkestone's first band, having started at the tender age of thirteen in 1958. Although fame never touched me on the shoulder, I still managed to have a fantastic time during the late fifties and sixties. I had rubbed shoulders with peers at school who were destined to hit the global road to fame. I had played in the school band with Noel Redding, who had international success with The Jimi Hendrix Experience, and Pete Kircher, who found fame initially with The Honeybus and later Status Quo. Well, to be honest, although I dreamed of being a rock star, fate dictated it was not to be! Music has always been a part of my life, and still is, to a significant degree. With the result, alongside a fellow conspirator, Ray Miller, we set up a Live Music Festival in the magnificent high North Pennines of England, which has gone from strength to strength since its inception in 2014. That is until the global pandemic said otherwise in 2020. One of the reasons my friendship with Hayley has survived over so many decades must be based on our initial meeting. Yes, I was hanging over a farm gate, talking to possibly the most famous Hayley on the planet, but we actually never conversed about Hayley Mills, the film star! We just talked about horses, in which we shared a common interest. From Hayley's point of view, it was probably refreshing to meet someone who saw past the celebrity image and saw the teenage girl playing with her horse. I'm sure all of us have experienced meeting a person for the first time, where we immediately feel comfortable in their presence. From the outset, I felt this was the case chatting with Hayley, as though we had known each other for years.

It has indeed been a unique experience. Hayley went on to lead her life in film, television and theatre, whilst I played with horses, transport, cabinet making and music! Joe, my son, encouraged me to write this story, based on these two entirely separate lives, which as I mentioned previously, have periodically crossed over in the correspondence we shared, and the times we have met. One of my dearest memories must be sitting alongside Hayley on a garden seat swing, when she lived in Hampton. The late afternoon sun shone. Crispian and Jason were charging around the garden, trying their best to squirt us with water from a squeegee bottle, whilst Hayley and I sipped wine and chatted.

1 NORTH AFRICA TO COWDEN

It is one of those strange quirks in life, where you set off on one particular path with the sweet innocence to see where your destination might lead you, but the ensuing encounters lead you to a fantastic 'wow' factor conclusion! So it was with me at the start of this remarkable story.

The year was 1958. I was just thirteen years old, and we all lived in a different era compared to the technological age we live in now! There were no computers or game consoles, which created the strange dichotomy that we are given a global aspect to our social needs, but stifled into a personal prison of our own bedroom! More like, life was spent outside, especially living in a town like Folkestone in Kent, which lies in the shadow of the North Downs escarpment and the famous White Cliffs of Dover. Apart from swimming and kayaking, it was the home of many of our walks and more adventurous games. From the summit of either Caesars Camp Hill, which now has the portal to the Channel Tunnel at its base, or the neighbouring Sugar Loaf Hill, you would look out across the town with its impressive Victorian viaduct, containing seven million bricks that span the wide and steep valley where the town nestles a stone's throw from the English Channel just beyond. On a clear day, the French coastline is visible, being just over twenty miles away. On a dull and overcast day on our side of the English Channel, but very bright and sunny in France, the summer colours of the French cornfields were distinct to the naked eye. This could prove useful when planning a day trip to Boulogne or Calais! Interestingly, Boulogne has its own Napoleon Column set on the cliffs facing the land he proposed to conquer! Unlike Nelson's column in Trafalgar Square, the French column has an internal spiral staircase. For those with a good head for heights, and who don't suffer from vertigo, the view is worth the effort! Unfortunately for Napoleon, he passed away before the column was completed!

The oddity about our three local Folkestone hills, Sugar Loaf Hill, Caesar's Camp Hill and Chimney Pot Hill, was the historic tank trap, which encircles them close to their summits. World War Two had come to an end just thirteen years earlier in 1945, during which Folkestone, being close to the Hawkinge Aerodrome, was a German target. The aerodrome housed a squadron of the famous Spitfires, who were on constant standby to fight the invading Luftwaffe. After the near catastrophe of Dunkirk in 1940, where a German invasion looked a distinct possibility (but again, in another sense, also the miracle of Dunkirk, where 300,000 British and Allied soldiers were rescued off the beaches under heavy and prolonged enemy attack), further defensive plans were created to protect our coastline. One of the results was the tank traps being carved out of the hills to act as a nuisance factor to the invaders. The nearby Royal Military Canal, which spans the length of the Romney Marsh, was constructed to keep Napoleon's armies at bay over a hundred and fifty years earlier in 1804. I grew up thinking all hills had these white chalk bands around their summits! There weren't many vehicles in the fifties, so apart from the odd time of being taken to London on a coach, my life centred around our corner of Kent, playing on these fabulous rolling downs, that end on the coastline known as the White Cliffs of Dover, with the sea being my playground too. Many of my early years have fond memories of being taken down the Warren, which was a section of the White Cliffs on the western end near Folkestone. There would be a great gaggle of aunts and uncles with their children, notwithstanding my mother, pop, and my two older sisters, all armed with sandwiches, flasks, and buckets and spades. We would have such fun exploring rock pools for crabs, or searching for iron pyrites more commonly known as 'fool's gold'. Folkestone suffered extensive damage during the war, so there were many bombed out houses to explore. However, as a child, you do not comprehend that people had got hurt or worse, lost their lives in these derelict buildings.

The war years gave us a plethora of war films made during, and after, the conflict, with many of the wartime productions produced as propaganda, to boost the nation's morale. Although computers were still a long way off for the masses, and television was in its infancy, we did have the big screen! The cinema industry was taking off in style. After weathering the wearisome long years of the war, the nation craved some entertainment to lift the spirits. The cinema industry rose to the challenge, especially in the fifties, by using the available technology of the period to develop the Cinemascope screen with its surround sound system! My first experience of this was a film called "The Robe" made in 1953, in glorious colour. It portrayed the story of Christ's crucifixion and starred Richard Burton, Jean Simmons, Victor Mature, Michael Rennie and many more giants of the silver screen of the time. It was a massive global success. The

American budget ran to four million dollars to produce the film, and it grossed thirty-six million dollars, which certainly in 1953 was a massive sum of money. I must confess to falling in love with the film industry, spending most Saturday afternoons in any of the four cinemas we were lucky enough to have in Folkestone. Sixpence (pre decimal) would secure you a half-decent seat in either The Odeon, The Central, The Playhouse, or The Savoy cinema, whereas with the threepenny seat, you would definitely need glasses!

My favourite and most memorable war film was without a doubt, "Ice Cold In Alex", written by Christopher Landon, produced in 1958, and starring John Mills, Anthony Quayle, Sylvia Syms and Harry Andrews. I had seen John Mills in many wartime films, such as "In Which We Serve", "We Dive at Dawn", "The Big Blockade" and of course, "Dunkirk" which was also filmed in 1958, but it was his depiction of Captain Anson in "Ice Cold in Alex" which actually started me on the path to meeting and becoming a lifelong friend of his youngest daughter Hayley.

The fifties and sixties were such vibrant and exciting times. In 1954, the rock'n'roll era burst on to the UK scene in the form of Bill Haley and The Comets performing their "Rock Around the Clock". The music scene just got to me, and I knew I had to be part of it! Everything was changing. The 'Teds' with their famous, but outrageous Edwardian fashion, complete with the obligatory skin tight, drainpipe jeans, and of course, topped with the famous 'Elvis' hairstyle laden with gel to keep it in position, all evolved in the fifties, much to the horror and anguish of many mums and dads. These were replaced in the sixties by the 'mods and rockers', which caused even more problems in many UK households and made newspaper headlines for all the wrong reasons. Lesley Hornby, better known as Twiggy, hit the headlines with her miniskirts, which probably caused many an argument between mums and their daughters, although the young men never complained! There seemed to be an air of freedom, not just in fashion and music, but also in our culture, where things were no longer accepted, but probed and questioned. Possibly all the result of the two world wars. Imagine my excitement in 1958, when my wish was granted, and I started playing the bass guitar at the ripe old age of thirteen. I was particularly drawn to the bass because it represented, alongside the drums, the power behind the rock sound, and created the platform for the lead guitar to do his fiddly bits, and the vocalist to warble his song! My parents very kindly purchased a Rossetti bass guitar with its deep blue body, and a small, fifteen watt Zenith amp, which are probably collectors pieces now, if they are still about! The pair came to twenty two pounds, a king's ransom in those days. Talking of which, I still own and play a 1963 Old Kraftsman, six string guitar made in New York. This brand of guitar was produced by the Kay Company, who started their musical enterprise in 1890. Interestingly, for the guitar aficionados, the model I own is a semi-acoustic, fitted with a pair of Gibson pickups. The fretboard is brilliant, especially using grade 9 strings. Even after an evening of string stretching performing, the guitar stays perfectly in tune! The guitar was given to me in 2005 by a local chap who had stored it in his attic for twenty-five years! It was given to him by a cousin who lived in New York. The story goes, the guitar had at one point landed around an American campfire during the 70's Vietnam war! An amazing jazz guitar with an equally amazing history! Certainly, a guitar I treasure and even to this day sits next to my armchair.

The Seekers were, I believe, Folkestone's first rock'n'roll band, consisting of lead guitarist Jeff Ratecliffe on a homemade electric guitar, Jim Williams, vocalist and rhythm guitar, my older cousin Mick O'Neil on drums and little old me on bass. Mick was my big hero, as he was an authentic 'Ted', and Jeff was a consummate Golden Virginia 'rollie' smoker. To the extent, even now, if I get a whiff of this brand, I am immediately transported back to that era! The year was 1958, which seemed to be proving a pivotal year! Fame never tapped me on the shoulder, but it certainly did for two of my contemporaries at the Harvey Grammar School in Folkestone. Apart from The Seekers rock band, I had by 1960 also played in the school band alongside Noel Redding, a phenomenal lead guitarist whose party trick was to stand in front of another guitarist and play their instrument! The drummer was a friend, Pete Kircher. Noel went on to have a global career, playing the bass with the legendary Jimi Hendrix in the Jimi Hendrix Experience. I believe one of the reasons Hendrix was drawn to Noel was his style of playing the bass. He was after all a consummate lead player with many years of experience. In many ways, he inspired many future bass players with his unique style. It fitted in so well with Jimi's innovative guitar skills. The whole Jimi Hendrix Experience sound was completed with Mitch Michell with his jazz influence on percussion. Pete, who incidentally lived five doors from me, had initial success with The Honeybus in 1968, but ultimately ended up, playing for Status Quo, where his last gig before retiring was the famous first "Live Aid Show" in 1985. Status Quo actually started the Wemberly event, performing their massive hit "Rocking All Over The World", which seemed relevant in the circumstances! Pete and the band were presented to Prince Charles after their performance. Sadly, Noel passed away in 2003 after living out his latter days in Clonakilty, Ireland, where he enjoyed the odd jam session, alongside a few of his old mates at the renowned De Barras Folk Club.

During August 1961, the film "No My Darling Daughter" produced by Betty E. Box, and written by Kaye Bannerman and Harold Brooke, hit the screens. It starred Michael Redgrave and Juliet Mills, Hayley's big sister. Anxious to have my sixpenny worth, I took myself off to enjoy the film at the Odeon cinema. Bearing in mind I was now sixteen with the possibility of the hormones stirred, I stared at the silver screen and fell in love with the delectable Juliet Mills playing her character, Tansy, in this romantic comedy. Of course, I felt insanely jealous of Rad Fulto and Michael Craig, who played Cornelius, and Thomas Barclay being her love interests! In my immature world, I decided there was no other course of action but to become famous in my own right, move in the same circles as Juliet, and eventually marry her! The old adage of "the best laid plans of mice and men" totally floored my ambitions, bringing my lovelorn dreams crashing down around my ears, especially since reading in a Kent newspaper the public announcement given by Mr and Mrs John and Mary Mills that their eldest daughter Juliet was to marry an American chap, Russell Alquist, in October 1961. The wedding was to be at St. Magdalene Church, in the picturesque village of Cowden in Kent. Well, there was no question in my mind. I would have to attend the event to witness for myself this sun drenched Adonis, for whom Juliet had actually forsaken me! To be fair, this was only one part of the reason I took myself off to Cowden. I had never seen anyone famous in my life, save only the young looking, freshly crowned Queen Elizabeth, in 1953, as she sped past us in her motorcade, along Shorncliffe Road in Folkestone. Being a child of eight years old, a small Union Jack flag was unceremoniously dumped in my hand, alongside all the other assembled schoolchildren, and we were instructed to wave with great gusto as the Queen drove past! We had waited with growing excitement for the moment when the young monarch would appear. In truth, that was exactly what it turned out to be, a moment! By the time I waved my flag, she was gone. However, I sensed that same excitement as I mounted the train for Tonbridge and proceeded to walk the ten miles or so to Cowden. The weather was sunny, and the countryside in that part of Kent was a joy to walk through with miles of leafy lanes, which gave me time to ponder on seeing my favourite pinup, and hopefully other famous characters from the film world. In the event, I was not disappointed. A very kind, elderly lady gave me a lift for the last three or four miles, which was most fortunate, as I apparently underestimated how long those ten miles would take to cover on foot. Indeed, I would have missed the wedding, which was set for early afternoon. In the event, our timing was impeccable, arriving just as wedding guests and local villagers assembled around the kissing gate to the early 14th Century St. Magdalene Church. I did not have long to wait before the guests started to arrive. The first car brought Kenneth More, who starred in the famous Betty E. Box film, "The Thirty Nine Steps", filmed just a few years ago in 1959 and penned by John Buchan. The next to arrive was Jack Hawkins, a veteran of the big screen, who starred in such films as "The Cruel Sea" and "Land of the Pharaohs". A steady stream of guests arrived, and wandered up the short walk to the church porch, before disappearing into its interior. In the background, I could hear the stirring organ music. A few minutes later, another chauffeur driven car arrived with Juliet's younger sister Hayley, accompanied by her mum, Mary Hayley Mills. Here were the actual family members! For the benefit of my teenage fan obsession, this was a seriously, big 'wow' moment! Both my hero from "Ice Cold In Alex" and the heroine from "No My Darling Daughter" would appear shortly! The tension was rising! Being her sister's bridesmaid, and newsworthy in her own right, the paparazzi immediately surrounded Hayley, coupled with a few guests, all hovering just beyond the kissing gate, waiting for the arrival of the bride and the bride's dad. In the meantime, Mary, having made sure Hayley's dress was still perfect, turned, and joined the congregation in the church. I never saw Russell Alquist arrive, but presumed he and the best man had entered earlier.

By 1961, Hayley had become the darling of the British nation at just fifteen years of age. The second Shirley Temple indeed! Two years earlier, Hayley had already won a BAFTA award for the most promising newcomer for the classic 1959 detective film "Tiger Bay" in which she starred alongside her famous Dad. On the back of that huge success, Hayley caught the notice of the legendary Walt Disney who signed her up to make a series of films under his Disney banner, with the first one being "Pollyanna" in 1960, followed by "The Parent Trap" in 1961, and "In Search of the Castaways" during 1962. In spite of appearing in the role of a bridesmaid for her sister's wedding and a major Hollywood film, Hayley also found time to star in the film "Whistle Down the Wind" in 1961, a story written by her mother. The poignant story of a group of children who thought they had found Jesus in a barn, but who had actually come across a wanted murderer! Bryan Forbes directed this British made film, which was filmed in black and white, which I found actually enhanced the grey atmospherics of the Pennine locations. I believe possibly, Mary Hayley Bell originally had the inspiration for the story while living at their Sussex House Farm in Cowden.

My attention was directed from staring at Hayley, who looked so incredibly pretty with her sun-drenched golden hair, to suddenly being aware there was an excited stir in the small crowd, as the car arrived with Juliet and her father! Their arrival heralded a round of applause from us onlookers. This was the pivotal moment; they were actually here for real. There was no longer the uncomfortable need to experience getting a neck ache from staring up at the big silver screen in the cinema! I was looking straight at them. Juliet looked so radiant as she alighted from the car. Both Juliet and John Mills paused for a moment in the churchyard posing for photographs, before they too disappeared into the shade of St. Magdalene porch, accompanied by Hayley in her role as bridesmaid. The small crowd around the church gate gradually dissipated into smaller groups, happily chatting about the invasion by the film world into their peaceful, idyllic corner of the British countryside. Some, I supposed, were very local and actually very used to seeing members of the Mills clan around the village, especially as they lived very close to their farm. Others, like me, would be keen film buffs, eager to come and see their favourite film star. Obviously, there would be a break for thirty minutes while the wedding service was being conducted. I used the time by sitting on one of the conveniently placed benches and munching on the sandwiches my mum had made for me. This gave me time to reflect on the situation. My wounded teenage heart had to face the fact that Juliet had finally "betrayed" me and dashed all my dreams and ambitions forever! She was actually getting married to another chap just a few yards away! Oh, the pain of it all! People sitting close to me probably thought I was shielding my eyes from the sun, but the reality was, I had my hand firmly pinned to my forehead in the traditional Shakespearean manner, "Woe is me, forsooth, I am so undone"! But then an epiphany wormed its way into my immature head, which somehow placated the misery! Against this amazing backdrop, where I not only had my favourite iconic actor, but also other household names!

To cap it all, I was in the presence of the quintessentially English rose in the shape of the delectable Hayley Catherine Rose Vivien Mills!

Oh, what a shallow, hormonal youth I was, shifting my allegiance so readily to the younger sister, just like that! But there you have it! That's life! The service had ended. The congregation emerged from the confines of the church once more into the sunshine, with the chimes of the church bells confirming the entrance of Mr. & Mrs Russell Alquist into their newly married status. I hovered to get a last glimpse of my lost love, and finally as the last car departed for the reception in the family's nearby farm, I turned for home.

The long trek back to the railway, and the train journey home, was much shrouded by the exciting and memorable events of the day, culminating in much intellectual consideration. The main thought being: "I really must watch a few of Hayley Mills' films!"

2 THE FIRST ENCOUNTER

After all the excitement of the outing to Cowden and boring all the members of my family and friends to exhaustion with the repetitive accounts of that day, life dropped back to normal. I continued schoolwork at the local Harvey Grammar School in Folkestone, whilst still pursuing my dream to become the next Cliff Richard. Ignoring the relevant fact that I could not actually sing. After The Seekers, I performed with a local rock'n'roll band, named The Mystics, which morphed into The Mixed Feelings. I was never a frontman, like I say, I couldn't sing to save my life! The only time I tried was at a holiday camp not far from Aberystwyth on the mid-Welsh coast, in 1960. A guitarist about the same age as me had stood up to perform, but suddenly got stage fright and did not want to sing "Living Doll", a record which was then riding high in the charts for Cliff Richard. I knew the words and he knew the chords, so off we went. I made a skilful job of murdering the song with my terrible rendition. Needless to say, I have never warbled anything since that painful performance! The audience clapped with enthusiasm, and to this day, I cannot imagine why, unless they cheered for the guitarist! Yes, great guitarist, shame about the singer! It must be said, playing in a band was great, especially viewing the audience from the stage, having great fun doing their rocking and rolling. It gave me such a buzz. Who wanted drugs when you had adrenaline coursing through your veins! The band's performing levels ran on high octane overdrive at most gigs. I have never smoked or indulged in illegal substances, despite knowing it was all around me. My drug was to play rock music!

The end of my scholastic career came in 1962. Still with the notion of becoming a professional bass player, but initially found myself working in an accountant's office in Folkestone, which lasted just three months. David Lye, a chartered accountant and my employer, was charming. However, a colleague, appointed as my supervisor, had been put on the planet purely to make my life a misery! My day consisted of adding pages and pages of figures into a ledger, followed by meticulously cross casting them to make them penny perfect. Of course, as soon as one ledger was completed, another appeared! There were no computers, and being the junior, I was not permitted to use the one and only handle driven adding machine in the entire building! The frustration was that apart from being locked into a lifestyle I didn't enjoy, the pay was lousy! I worked a forty eight hour week for three pounds a week!. The temptation, after three months of this treadmill existence, was to gaze out of the window and daydream of rock'n'roll! The powers that be had noticed. One day, Mr Lye called me into his office to kindly suggest I find alternative employment, adding I could stay until another job could be found. In one sense, it wasn't about the money. Every Friday and Saturday, I played with The Mixed Feelings, regularly earning twelve pounds and ten shillings per gig! My parents, however, pointed out very succinctly that I needed a stable career, as the music would be a mere passing phase! The other frustration was that my contemporaries, the two friends I had performed with in the school band, were determined to become rock legends, and earned their rite of passage by playing around Europe. It was a hard road to fame, existing in a van touring for weeks at a time, without much money or clean clothes, but obviously it paid off for Pete and Noel. Interestingly, near the end of my school career, I found myself behind Pete in the queue, waiting to chat to the careers officer about our career choices. He went into his meeting wanting to be a professional rock drummer and came out wanting to be a signwriter! He worked for a Folkestone sign writing company for a short period, before the open roads of Europe led him to the subsequent fame. After leaving Status Quo in 1985, he apparently returned to his old trade of sign writing and set up his own business. In the early days, when we both lived near each other in Cheriton, which is close to the channel tunnel site, I can remember Pete arriving on my doorstep with drum sticks in his hands, but no drums. He would make do with cardboard boxes and saucepans to hone his skills as a budding percussionist! One of Pete's strange quirks, which I never fathomed out, featured with apples! If you produced and ate an apple whilst he was playing the drums, he would crease up with laughter and fall apart! In 1968, when he was riding high in the charts with The Honeybus and "Can't Let Maggie Go", I went to see him perform at the renowned Leas Cliff Hall in Folkestone. After squeezing my way through the audience to the front of the stage, I produced my big shiny apple and proceeded to munch! Pete noticed me, and professionally turned his head away from me, but not before mouthing two words which rhyme with 'Trucking Banker'!

Noel went on to be a massive star with the Jimi Hendrix Experience. The connection with Noel led to my amazing 'experience' too, but more of that later! Apart from the music, I used to hang out with Noel and his sister Vicky, down the Horn Street Park, where they lived at the Seabrook end of Scene Valley, close to the sea, and I lived in Cheriton at the top end of the valley, where the Channel Tunnel terminus is situated.

As fame was not knocking on my door anytime soon, and probably due to the fact that I liked my home comforts too much, it was time to pursue another career! Of course, the overriding factor was Mr Lye's advice to abandon my failing accountancy work and pursue a more suitable job. This was a positive move. I have always loved the countryside, so I was lucky to become a records clerk on a large three and half thousand acre farm near Ashford in Kent. I took the view that if I couldn't be a rock sensation, then option two would be to work with animals!

The owner of this large estate was the industrialist Rudy Sternberg, who seldom visited the farm save only for a two week vacation in the summer and a week at Christmas. He was a hugely successful business man with an extraordinarily charismatic character. He was born in Torun, Poland, and moved to Britain before the second world war, in 1937, to study chemical engineering at the London University. After Germany invaded Poland in 1939, Rudy joined the British army, but was demobilised four years later on health grounds. Due to the Nazi regime persecuting the Jews in Europe, he lost his family, except for one brother, who joined him in Britain. In 1945, Rudy became a British subject. Using his newly acquired chemical engineering knowledge and his natural flair for business, he started producing plastic buttons on a small scale. His success was meteoric. By 1948, he had acquired a factory in Manchester to produce the revolutionary Bakelite, a plastic substance conceived in 1909 by the chemist Leo Baekeland. Rudy became one of the biggest plastic producers in the UK, under his banner of the Sterling Group of companies, also established in 1948. By the time I arrived on his farm at Shadoxhurst in 1962, Rudy Sternberg was a multi-millionaire. Not only did he own twelve farms across the Romney Marsh, which stretched up to the North Downs in Kent, but he also owned Britain's biggest export company, United Dominions Export. He also had banking interests, construction ventures, and even potash mines in Eastern Europe.

One of the advantages of this job was the attractive twenty mile journey to work each day from Folkestone to Shadoxhurst, which followed the scenic route that meanders along the old Ham Street Road, on the edge of the Romney Marsh, encompassing such picturesque villages as Ruckinge, Billsington and Bonnington. A few centuries earlier, smugglers would bring their contraband along this route, on the way to the famous Slippery Sam Inn on Stone Street, not too far from Canterbury. The big bonus to this new job was that I had my own office! The Sternberg Farm, estate office, was a modern timber chalet construction, housing a spacious open area with a reception area, plus two other offices, one being mine and one being for the farm secretary, Miss Ivy Fountain. This lady I found to be wonderfully eccentric. She had no background in farming whatsoever, but was a retired writer and journalist, having been the sub-editor for a national newspaper during the war. Rudy Sternberg and Ivy Fountain were old friends, both equally flamboyant in their view on life. As he wanted someone to oversee the twelve different farm managers which made up the estate, Sternberg managed to entice his old friend out of her retirement to be the overall manager and make the farm more centralised! I recall that even my interview did not follow normal protocol! One of the first questions shot at me was, "can you make a cup of tea?" Agreeing to anything to make an impression, I was directed to the little kitchen, where she instructed me by shouting in an incredibly booming voice from the next office, on how to make a proper cup of China tea with a twist of lemon! A couple of seconds elapsed before she bellowed at me to make another one for myself, but use the ordinary tea and not the China variety! The interview went in the same vein. She was dismissive of the seven 'O'level GCEs and one 'A' level I had achieved through actually quite hard study, being in the 'd' stream throughout my time at the Harvey Grammar School! At the end of each answer I gave, all I got was a series of long "mmm's", but finally the interview ended with, "I'd rather see what you can do, and can you start next Monday?"

I was to be in the office at 8.30am sharp and watch out for Miss Fountain at 9.00am to appear from the bungalow around the corner, where she lived. She was easily distinguishable, as she was a walking contradiction! An incredibly loud and colourful character who perpetually hummed equally loud unrecognisable melodies, but with a dress sense slightly at odds with her persona. She was very tweedy. Her skirt and jacket were made of a heavy brown coloured plaid. Her stockings were thick and brown too, with brown brogues to match. The only colour was a cream, or sometimes, pink neckerchief, which folded neatly into her jacket. Her ageing craggy face could best be described as well-worn with life. To complete the picture, she wore a pair of heavy horn-rimmed glasses, which suited her short hair and face well. Apart from her clothing, there was no mistaking Miss Fountain's gait as she strode towards the Estate office in a strange bow-legged manner! She seemed to sway from side to side as she strode forward to the office. To be fair, Shadoxhurst, where the estate office was situated, is an incredibly quiet and small village with a very limited population. In that context, anyone would stand out, especially in the morning! As soon as Miss Fountain came into view, I was to prepare and make sure her China tea with a twist of lemon was in place on her desk! She suggested it might be a good idea to introduce myself to the other two local women who worked in the office, when they arrived, and make them a cuppa too!

The Sternberg Estate was an impressive collection of farms, each independently run by a manager. Plurenden Manor Farm housed the Friesian herd of cattle for producing the milk, complete with four fierce Friesian Bulls to keep the supply chain going. The large white pig herd had their home at the Harlakenden Farm, where two hundred and fifty sows bred their progeny to be taken to pork and bacon weight. There were six boars to aid and abet the sows! Some five hundred Romney Marsh ewes, popular for their wool, roamed on the vast blustery Marshes, the cycle of life served by four rams. The estate office itself was situated next to Park Farm and home to the Aberdeen Angus breed. There was, but one Angus gentleman, named Newhouse Edwin Elliot, who served the ladies on Park Farm! He weighed in at one ton! He was incredibly docile, which actually was a problem. He enjoyed trying to rub himself on you, which potentially could prove incredibly dangerous! They built a ramp for Newhouse to serve his ladies, as he could otherwise damage their backs with his amorous intentions! The other farm units dealt with the arable side of the enterprise. The job was totally absorbing, as I was responsible for all the milk records, to determine which bull to put to which cow to produce the best yield of milk. The same applied to all the other animals. Every field had its own record to keep. This would add to the historic use of the acreage, showing whether oat, wheat or barley seeds were being sown, cultivated and harvested, recording the tonnage each field produced. On top of this, various types of potatoes were grown. The recording was non-stop. I spent very little time in the office, as I was so busy driving between the various farms, collecting the necessary information to collate back at the office towards the end of the day. The various managers, especially on the animal side, were people who had worked the land all their lives. I would advise which bull to put with an appropriate cow, and the herdsman manager would just grin and tell me "it's already done mate!". They carried all this information in their heads!

After making sure Miss Fountain's obligatory cup of China tea, complete with its lemon twist, was ready on this particular summer morning in 1963, I was summoned to Miss Fountain's office, by the customary bellow from the adjoining office:

"Trevor, I have a very important job for you today. You don't have much on today?" she asked, but without waiting for any reply, "No? Well, that is excellent, as I have some important Aberdeen Angus pedigree records to deliver to the manager at the Mills' farm over at Cowden".

These two magic trigger words saw me go into some immediate sort of comatose mental shutdown! 'Mills' and 'Cowden'! My ears refused to believe what I was hearing! These two words were irretrievably locked together in my immature head since the wedding two years earlier.

"Trevor! Are you okay? Do you need to sit down or something?" were the first discernible words that penetrated the mist that seemed to blur my vision!

"Er. No Miss Fountain. I am fine. It is just that I have always been a huge fan of John Mills, the actor who starred in the film "Ice Cold In Alex", and by chance I happen to know he has a farm in Cowden!" Which was in part the truth, but I had delicately sidestepped the untenable fact, I was desperately infatuated with his younger daughter, as were millions of other lovesick males around the world!

"Yes, I agree Trevor, bloody good film, saw it a few years ago! Ah, so you are a John Mills fan, in which case I must wag my professional finger at you! If by any chance, you come across ANY member of the family, you do NOT approach them on any pretext. Do you understand?"

"Yes Miss Fountain". Although her voice was firm, there was a glimmer of a smile hovering around her mouth and a mischievous glint in her eye! She was clearly thinking, as were the two other female colleagues in the outer office, "Who does he think he is kidding! He is obviously in love with Hayley Mills, aren't they all?" At this point, Hayley was at the top of her game, given her age at the time was just seventeen, and with several globally successful films in the bag. Her fan base at that time far exceeded even a new and upcoming band called The Beatles, a group from Liverpool, whose sound revolutionised the music world. You may have heard of them!

"Right, here are the records to take to the farm manager. The farm address is on the front. Here is a receipt for him to sign to say he has safely received the package. Any questions? No? Good! Get yourself a cup of tea before you go, and oh, whilst you are at it, perhaps you could make one for me and the ladies out there!"

"Absolutely!" was all I could muster as I fled to the kitchenette to prepare the refreshments. Floating on air did not explain how I felt! Needless to say, I gulped the tea down as quickly as the scalding liquid would allow before turning to the estate office door.

"Oh Trevor! Haven't you forgotten something? What about the bloody package?"

"Oh, absolutely Miss Fountain" I replied, catching the box file that was winging its way through the air in my direction!

"One more thing Trevor, fill your car up at the Manor and

get a chitty from Mr. Ballard. Enjoy your day, see you tomorrow!"

As soon as the door closed behind me, I heard the hysterical cackling of the three women in the office! The insane laughter still ringed in my ears when I drove into the grounds of the manor house known as Plurenden Manor, the country residence belonging to Rudy Sternberg. A beautiful example of a black and white, timber framed house of the Tudor era, complete with it's low Kent peg tiled roof and tall brick chimney stacks. The Manor and the adjacent farm were just a few miles from the village of High Halden. Mr Ballard was the gardener and general caretaker for the manor and its extensive grounds. He also held the key to the farm fuel pumps. Having filled the tank, signed for the fuel and been issued with the requisite receipt, I turned the bonnet of my trusty old 1954 Ford Prefect in the direction of Cowden, just some fifty five miles distant. It was a glorious summer day, with brave Helios shining down, with only a few passing clouds to break up the constant hue of the sky. Mind you, the only cloud on my horizon was cloud nine! Here I was being sent on legitimate farm business to the Mills family home! Of course, I constantly reminded myself they probably would not be there. They would be way too busy rehearsing or filming in some exotic location. The Wealden villages floated by in the mists of my anticipation. St. Michaels, Biddenden, Sissinghurst, Goudhurst, then skirting around Tunbridge Wells and on to Langton Green via the A264, until finally turning left into Hartsfield Road, leading to my destination. I pulled up outside the Church, where just two years ago I witnessed the Mills wedding procession arriving with their guests. The first person I asked for directions knew exactly where Sussex House Farm was, so within a few minutes, I slid through the farm gates where the object of my dreams lived! In my teenage mind, Juliet had taken the back seat, and although their dad was still a brilliant actor, he was not, well, Hayley! After a couple of stops, I was finally directed to the farm estate car park, where I left the vehicle. Winding round several outbuildings, I finally arrived at the manager's home, and if I correctly recall, was aptly named "Hayley Cottage". I was greeted with a warm welcome, and given a cup of tea and a plate of sandwiches, which were most welcome. Having passed the pedigree letters to the manager, he immediately studied them before adding they had expected me, as Miss Fountain had phoned ahead. He was interested in learning about the various breeding policies regarding Rudy Sternberg's farms, and in particular quizzed me over my job title of Farm Record Clerk. Of course, my head was buzzing more about the owner of Sussex House Farm, or rather his younger daughter, while sipping tea, but I managed to remain professional and avoided all mention of the Mills family. The vision of Miss Fountain and her wagging finger kept me on the straight and narrow! The convention of polite withdrawal is usually at the point where either party discreetly looks at their watch, possibly two or three times, before exclaiming, almost with alarm, "Gosh, is that the time?" Clearly, this was the signal for me to depart, as the manager peered at his watch! We shook hands, and he wished me a safe journey back. As I turned to meander through the outbuildings, towards the estate car park, I felt a slight pang of despair, as I had not seen anyone connected to the Mills family. So near and yet so far! Then it happened! I turned the last corner and there she was! That mass of golden hair and cherub nose was instantly recognisable! There was Hayley hanging over the field gate, making a fuss of her pony. What a dilemma! Do I obey the wagging finger command of my boss, or do I approach and introduce myself? Weighing up the situation, it occurred to me that

Miss Fountain was about fifty-five miles away, no doubt sipping China tea. Hayley Mills, the girl of my adolescent dreams, was standing a few feet away!

"Hi, is this your pony?" I enquired in a somewhat high pitched voice. Hayley half turned and brushed her windswept hair from her face.

"Yes, she is rather beautiful, isn't she?"

"What is her name?"

"Annabelle", she replied, and that was the start of a conversation that has carried us through to the present day. From the first few words, we found a common thread by talking about horses. Apart from music, my other passion was horses, having ridden since the age of nine. I regaled Hayley with some wonderful anecdotes concerning the two charismatic, twin elderly sisters, both called Miss Tywman, who ran The Prospect Riding Stable in the middle of Hythe. Stories of pony treks that took us through the leafy wooded grounds of Saltwood Castle, where in 1170 the four knights conspired to murder Thomas Becket, then the Archbishop of Canterbury in his Cathredral. Hayley laughed when I told her the first time I ever cantered was actually in the grounds of the castle! I was only nine years old, when Miss Twyman, on this occasion, had come alongside on her horse and asked whether I had ever experienced a canter?. I replied I had not. Instantly, she gave Whisky the piebald pony I was precariously perched on, a tap on the rear end with her crop, adding the command, "Hey up, Whisky, off you go!"Immediately, Whisky went into full pelt overdrive, with me clinging on for dear life to the ponies flying mane! The only crumb of comfort in the rapidly fading voice of Miss Tywman was her yelling:

"Don't worry Trevor, if you fall off, the ground comes up to meet you, so you only fall half the distance!"

How I managed to stay on, I have absolutely no clue! Both feet had come out of the stirrups, and like I say, I ended up clinging on to Whisky's mane as I had lost the reins. I must confess to uttering several expletives I should not have been aware of at the age of nine, but needs must, when needs must! After what seemed like a lifetime, my mount came to rest at the next field gate and promptly stuck his head down to munch the grass. With the consequence, I was suddenly pulled forward and gently slipped down his neck to the ground!

The time talking with Hayley passed almost as fast as Whisky had, but in many ways I actually had grown up in that first meeting. The conversation flowed so well, with no mention of her amazing film career or her fame, or indeed her famous family. As we chatted, the importance of seeing the person behind the face became abundantly clear. Like the old adage, don't judge a book by its cover. Like millions of others, I had come to adore the image and her status, and suddenly I was confronted with a kind and considerate person who, although articulate in conversation, displayed a charming shyness, which I found appealing. There was, in her shyness, a glimpse of a bird who wanted to be free and let her hair fly to the sound of the fiddle.

The conversation abruptly ended when a voice echoed across the field calling Hayley's name.

"It's best I go, I am being called," she said, sticking her hand out to politely shake mine. "I've enjoyed our chat."

"Me too Hayley, perhaps we'll catch up at some point."

"Maybe, who knows". With a smile, she turned towards the floating voice and was gone!

I had the strange surreal sensation of being in some sort of dream, and at any moment the alarm on my bedside clock would eject me swiftly from the nocturnal-like stupor into the reality of breakfast and work! But no, here I was, still sitting in my car staring out through the front screen, in the farm carpark in Cowden! The last twenty to twenty-five minutes had been no dream, but reality!

Needless to say, I had absolutely no recollection of driving back to Folkestone. The car went into some sort of automatic pilot. My mind was constantly evaluating the day's events, especially the conversation with Hayley. It begged the question, was that chat a one-off experience, and that would be the end of it? You met her, talked with her, which was more than most fans do, and now what? I felt a pang of anti-climax creeping over me! Indeed, I had by chance met her, almost like a scene out of one of her own Disney films, but my reality was working on the farm during the day, then rehearsing and performing with The Mixed Feelings on weekends. It made me wonder whether Hayley had experienced the same type of emotion. She had already experienced a sensational period of success, being catapulted into the international spotlight, where the paparazzi constantly followed her to snap photographs, and people forever pushing a piece of paper under her nose to sign her autograph! Perhaps it was refreshing too for her to talk to someone who not only shared her passion for horses, but never mentioned anything connected with her famous family or the film world to which she belonged.

Of course, there is nothing like a dose of reality to keep your feet firmly on the ground! My mother and father were excited by the fact I had met Hayley, but fell into the same trap as my female colleagues would do the following day in the farm office. They asked whether I had got her autograph, or quizzed her about "Pollyanna", whether she had met Walt Disney. Several friends asked a similar question, and when I answered 'no', my story of visiting Sussex House Farm and meeting up with Hayley was suddenly put into the realms of fantasy!! To be fair to Miss Fountain, I had flouted her instruction not to approach any member of the Mills's family, but she was genuinely pleased I had experienced such an encounter. After a few moments of listening to me, the topic swiftly moved to making more China tea, and to the question, had I sent off the monthly Large White Pig progeny records to P.I.D.A.? Goodbye cloud nine, hello ground!

3 THE IN-BETWEEN YEARS

After all the excitement of the Cowden encounter, life settled down again to a normality of work at the farm, tempered with playing in The Mixed Feelings, a band growing popular in the East Kent area. One of my personal favourite venues was "The Maritime Club", just off Snargate Street in Dover. In 1965, Martha and the Vandellas released their hit single, "Dancing in the Street". We did a cover version during that summer. The club hall was crammed with youngsters, so much so that the double doors were opened, and true to the lyrics of the song, they were dancing in the street! It was a brilliant experience. Two young entrepreneurial men had set up a circuit of various venues across East Kent. It was your choice to opt in or out. It could guarantee a gig every week, where each of the bands would reappear on the seventh week, which also meant the youngsters would never get bored with your sound. These gigs were organised in venues ranging from village halls, theatres, sport halls and clubs mainly on a Saturday night. This left a spare day on Friday to cover parties and other gigs. Mind, charming as the two men were, they were tough on timekeeping, one strike and you were toast! Although the idea was good, and we occasionally dipped our toe in, we tended to find our own gigs. Talking of which, we encountered a major problem performing at the local Odeon one Saturday morning for the children. During the scheduled films, there would be a thirty minute break where a local band would appear. The Mixed Feelings had performed once or twice, and I have to say, it was usually absolutely bedlam! It was noisy enough when the films were on, but when a live band appeared, the screaming went stratospheric! On the day in question, the band followed the normal routine of playing a couple of instrumental melodies as a warm up, before the vocalist bounced onto the stage to start rocking! Sadly, the singer was chatting up some female in the wings, consequently missing his cue! To make matters worse, our drummer, a chap not known for mincing his words, yelled across the stage to get the singer's attention. If remembered correctly, I believe the term as mentioned in a previous anecdote included the following: "You trucking tanker, get your trucking pass over here!" In the heat of the moment, the drummer had failed to notice his PA mic was still on! His little display of the list of expletives had been broadcast across the whole cinema! This was a catastrophic oops moment! A silence fell over the theatre. Personally, looking down at the rows of shocked young children, I was truly hoping a hole in the stage would appear to jump in! Probably in today's climate, the shock value would not have been so strong, but this was the sixties, and there were very young children in the audience. Having recovered, we finished our set, but needless to say, the band was summoned to the manager's office immediately afterwards, where we were collectively vilified, followed swiftly being sacked without pay! This was a valuable lesson in stagecraft and how to remain professional at all times.

Sadly, there was another unfortunate slip from grace in the sixties, when performing at the prestigious "Witchdoctor" Club in Hastings. The venue from it's high vantage point, had a beautiful view of the English Channel. This scenario involved symbols, a rather posh restaurant on the next level down, and an extremely angry restaurant manager! The footnote to this unfortunate anecdote was that we were not allowed to perform the second half of the evening and asked to leave! However, the drummer was allowed to remain with the band, mainly as he was an outstanding musician!

Thankfully, the Mixed Feelings were not responsible on one occasion, whilst supporting a well known sixties band in Margate, Kent. We had done our spot as the warmup act. The main band got about half way through their brilliant set when all mayhem broke out! The vocalist had selected a girl in the audience to make eye contact with, while doing a love song. Her boyfriend took exception to this overture, mounted the stage, and promptly attacked the singer! Well, that was it! All his local mates piled onto the stage and commenced a glorious punch up! Me, plus my own band members, looked on in dismay, as our guitars were still on the stage and could be used as weapons. We made a united decision to rush on, grab our instruments and rush off again! In the event, the security guards stopped the show until order had been restored and a few youngsters had been removed from the premises! It's all rock'n'roll!

During the summer of 1966, I had a little rock'n'roll moment myself. As a demonstration of defiance against the natural order of things, and alongside a girlfriend at the time, we decided to declare the Unilateral Declaration of Independence as a direct copycat to the UDI declared by Ian Smith in Rhodesia the previous year. Mind, our grand gesture was a local roundabout in the Folkestone area! The roundabout made a suitable 'island', containing a few trees and bushes to hide our camping presence! Putting up a flagpole with a union jack to herald our takeover was not the wisest of moves. It swiftly came to the attention of the much liked, local PC 'Big Ben', who was doing his daily rounds on his bike! He earned the affectionate title due to his height, especially with the helmet!

The ensuing conversation was swift and succinctly made!

"Oy, you two oiks, what do you think you are doing?" Ignoring our plea for compensation for trespassing on our island and declining an invitation to mediate, the PC continued by giving the ultimatum,

"I'll give you five minutes to bloody move your tent, flagpole, plus, all your other stuff, and bloody move off! D'yer get my drift? If you are still here when I get back, I'm taking you both down the nick."

The sight of his penetrating stare from such a lofty peak, plus his brisling moustache, was enough to make us immediately crumble and abandon our plans for the roundabout UDI!

After the visit to Cowden, I had sent Hayley a short letter, accompanied by a small water colour picture I had painted of her astride her pony, using the reasonable pass in 'A' level Art I had acquired in 1962. To be fair, I had copied it from a magazine photo, but it was a fair attempt, even if I do say it myself! There was a slight pang of disappointment when I received a solitary black and white photograph with her signature, but without any correspondence. Hayley was enjoying global success at that point with film releases such as "The Moonspinners", "The Chalk Garden" and "Summer Magic" and many more. The newspapers of that time had a field day speculating who was dating the darling of the Disney world! Hayley went on a dinner date once with the Beatle, George Harrison, but apparently it was a charity function her mother, Mary, had organised, and he was

Hayley's escort. I believe they went onto a club, but it was all innocent, especially as he had already met his future wife, Pattie, who he married in January 1966. However, Hayley's life took a dramatic change of direction in that year. She was contracted to make a film called "The Family Way", a story written by Bill Naughton, but originally entitled "All In A Good Time". The film co-starred her Dad, John Mills, and also Hywel Bennet. It was directed by Roy Boulting and produced by his brother, John Boulting. These twin brothers had carved out a considerably successful run during the fifties and sixties, making dozens of popular films under their Charter Films label, which started in 1937 with "The Landlady", followed swiftly by "Consider Your Verdict" in 1938. These two productions started their remarkable career in films, spanning several decades, becoming synonymous with classic drama and comedy, such as "Brighton Rock" and "Private's Progress". The critics considered "I'm All Right Jack", made in 1959, one of the Boulting brothers' finest satirical films.

Hayley was now an adult twenty year old, who had been making films since she was twelve. Therefore, she enjoyed the adulation from her huge fan base around the world, especially concerning the image created during the Disney years. "The Family Way", was selected as the film for Hayley to bridge the childhood transition to adulthood. Personally, I thought the film was a brilliant reflection of a young couple experiencing the problems of starting their marriage in the groom's parents' house, with a lack of privacy, which resulted in the newlyweds experiencing problems consummating their marriage. John Mills and Marjorie Rhodes excelled as Mr and Mrs Fitton, the groom's parents, as did John Corner and Avril Angers, portraying Mr and Mrs Piper, the bride's parents. The professional acting chemistry between Hayley and Hywel Bennet became abundantly clear as the film progressed. It was a financial success, and considered one of the finest films the 'terrible twins' had directed and produced. However, a gamble was taken with the inclusion of the famous scene where Hayley's character stands up clutching a towel around herself, having had a bath in the front room, when suddenly her brother-in-law enters. This was interesting, the whole film was in essence a story surrounding the subject of sex, but there was no sex or nudity scene involved other than the bath scene, where Hayley stands up and exposes her naked bottom to the camera. I considered this more of a statement on lack of privacy with home sharing, rather than a move to cause titillation for the audience. The film was certainly a landmark, or even possibly a crossroad epiphany for Hayley, in more ways than one. For me, the film worked perfectly. It was a brave choice, resulting in the right transitional route for Hayley to cross the child to adult divide. She will not only be remembered for her early films, but also created a launching platform for her highly successful adult career. For Hayley, the production had a life-changing consequence. She developed a relationship with the director Roy Boulting, who was thirty three years her senior, and after a two year engagement, resulted in their marriage in 1971. They married secretly in the south of France, which was a massive blow to the Mills' close knit family, as they were not invited! Apparently Roy did not want the attention of the media. Many years later, Sir John Mills covers this poignant period of their family life in his autobiography, "Up In The Clouds, Gentlemen Please", where he predicted the age difference could present a problem. He supposed there could always be the possibility Hayley might meet and fall in love with someone nearer her own age. Sadly, Hayley and Roy divorced in 1977 after just six years. However, their union did see the birth of Hayley's first son, Crispian, who was to go on to great things in the music business, being the front man for Kula Shaker in the late nineties.

During this period of the in-between years, my life was also turning in various twists and turns. At the end of 1964, I got the order of the boot from the job I loved, as the farm record clerk at Rudy Sternberg's Farm. The farm had hit a low point from a financial perspective, where it was found to be expedient to lighten the staff members. I had seriously enjoyed the Sternberg experience and have many fond memories, especially considering a gateway was created to meet Miss Mills! Some Saturdays on my day off would be spent on one of the twelve farms, becoming part of the family by mucking in to help with the various aspects of farming, whether animal stock or arable. I would arrive early in time for the farmhouse breakfast, and then off we would troop to muck out and feed animals, or harvest everything from potatoes to wheat, barley or oats. We would have sandwiches and flasks of tea sitting on a bale in the summer sun. It was indeed a glorious time! On one occasion, in the heart of the Romney Marsh, we sat on the deck of a cabin cruiser Rudy had purchased at the Earls Court Boat Show in London, and was stored in a barn on one of his farms! On another occasion, I experienced his kind generosity. I had just pulled up into the Farm Estate car park with my old Ford Prefect when I noticed Rudy was already there, presumably to share china tea with Miss Fountain and have farm conversations.

"Trevor, Trevor, come over here", he called in his distinctive clipped accent, and beckoning me with his hands, he said, "Rudy would like to talk with you."

I duly trotted over to where he stood, thinking "oh dear, what have I done wrong?"

"Good morning Mr.Sternberg", I said in a bright and cheery voice.

"Trevor, Trevor, is that your car?" he asked, nodding in the direction of my old banger.

"Yes, it is Mr. Sternberg."

"It smokes a bit, doesn't it?" he enquired, but before I could answer, he continued, "You use it on farm business?"

"Yes, apart from travelling between the farms, I also take Miss Fountain into Ashford every Friday to collect the farm wages". What I did not mention here was that I used to cringe at times on these Ashford excursions, as Miss Fountain would embark on her usual habit of bursting loudly into song, whether waiting in the queue at the bank or the local stationers. All embarrassing, especially when you are nineteen!

"Mmm… Trevor, Trevor, this is what Rudy will do for you. Take your car to any garage and get a new engine and gearbox, and Rudy will pay for it!" There was a slight pause before he continued,

"Yes?"

"Well, that's incredibly kind of you, Mr. Sternberg." I replied in my trailing voice, finding I was actually addressing his back, as he immediately turned and disappeared into the shadows of the office porch! He was true to his word and paid ninety-six pounds for a new engine and gearbox for my trusty, but somewhat rusty, 1954 Ford Prefect.

Sadly, during 1964, I turned my old Ford out of Rudy Sternberg's Estate Office car park for the last time. But as my mother always taught me, one door shuts and another will open, and lady luck was indeed smiling on me, or so I thought. By sheer chance, the week I was laid off from the farm, I found and secured work, doing exactly the same job as a farm record clerk on a much smaller unit nearer home. Oddly enough, would you believe part of my duties was to make china tea with a twist of lemon! The word lemon was the correct definition for the job. It was a complete disaster from the word go! The lady who owned the farm lived in a beautiful Georgian house adjacent to the farm. She and the manager clearly disliked each other with equal intensity. Unfortunately, I became the go-between in their constant war! Invariably, my opening line to either party when sent on an errand would be, “Don't shoot the messenger”. I got harangued on both sides, which finally culminated in the farm manager, in a pique of sheer anger, picking up and throwing a pitch fork in my direction! Fortunately, I had the good sense to duck as it whistled past me and embedded itself into the haystack behind me! I looked at the red-faced manager, then the pitchfork, and decided to remove myself from their employment, with immediate effect! Which I did! Went straight up to the farm office, rounded up a few personal effects, said goodbye to the farm owner, who stood with her mouth open, shocked that someone dared to quit the luxury of working for her! Strangely enough, their appalling attitude actually sharpened my ambition to work for myself and be in charge of my own destiny! Thus, I went self-employed from 1965 to 2010, when I officially retired. In so many ways, these two rotten tomatoes created a far better future for me! A fitting legacy must be the time the ‘Lady’ of the House instructed me to inform all the farming staff, under no circumstances were they allowed to use her drive to see her at the big house. In future, they would have to divert to the rear entrance, which was a considerably longer route. The following morning, as I arrived at the farm, I was met with the spectacle of the ‘Lady’ rushing around in her dressing gown, chasing and screaming at the twenty or so sows who were happily grazing and rolling on the front lawn! Karma presents itself in many forms!

Apart from the debacle of my recent departure from the employed fraternity, the music scene continued through the sixties. The Mixed Feelings were still active on the Kent circuit, resulting in an amazing experience one evening in December 1966, at the now demolished Hillside Club, just off the Folkestone town centre. This grey imposing building had a selection of shops on the ground level, with the Hillside Social Club on the second floor. This venue was regularly used by members of local bands who would meet to have a jam session, and perhaps a drink or three! By 1966, there had been a proliferation of bands eager to have their day in the sun. As mentioned before, I had played with an old chum, Noel Redding, in the school band in the early sixties. Interestingly, in my early days of The Seekers, I tried to persuade the other members to have Noel join our band. He came along to a rehearsal, but they declined him on his height. They thought he was too small, would you believe! The Seekers' loss was the world's gain! After leaving school, he joined forces with my other chum, Pete Kircher, and with various musicians, formed a group called The Strangers, which morphed into The Lonely Ones, The Burnettes and the Loving Kind. They went on to tour across Europe and earned their rite of passage by honing their stagecraft, playing the night clubs, especially in the Hamburg area. It was at this time in 1965, fame came knocking on Noel's door in the shape of Jimi Hendrix, who had previously worked, during the fifties as a session musician with many bands on the U.S. music scene, such as Little Richard and The Isley Brothers. It was Chas Chandler, the record producer and member of The Animals's sixties pop group, who recognised Jimi Hendrix's combined, jaw dropping guitar talent, and awesome stage presence. Chas managed to convince Jimi into, trying his luck by coming over to the UK. Noel had heard about this amazing guitarist, so applied for an audition in London. I think the appeal for Hendrix was that Noel, like himself, was a lead guitarist of considerable skill, but utilised and adapted that skill to the bass guitar. Actually, on one recording of "Red House", Noel swapped with Hendrix and played lead guitar. At school, Noel's party trick was to stand in front of another guitarist and play a melody on that musician's guitar! Quite an impressive skill to watch! Noel's talent on lead guitar had actually brought a whole new dimension to the bass instrument, which others have emulated over the decades. To complete the trio, Jimi had also engaged Mitch Mitchell, a London based drummer of diverse percussion techniques. He played everything from psychedelic rock through jazz to blues. Jimi, with Noel and Mitch, became the Jimi Hendrix Experience, and embarked on a global career, accumulating many massive hits under their belts, including, "Hey Joe", "Purple Haze", "All Along The Watchtower" and many more.

My experience happened at one of the jam sessions on New Year's Eve in 1966, when several local musicians had gathered at the Hillside Club. What a surprise, when Noel unexpectedly turned up with Jimi in tow, resulting in an amazing evening which took on a whole new dimension! It was a memorable session playing alongside Jimi, especially having recently released their massive hit "Hey Joe" in the October of 1966. It was awesome to listen to the magic of Jimi's guitar skills. He played several acoustic songs, including songs I had never heard before. Totally magic! I was lucky enough to sit with him and Noel when I managed to snatch a moment with him. He came across as quiet to the point of almost being shy, which was a complete contrast to his stage persona! A total contradiction to his flamboyant dress style and the music genre he played! Apart from talking about guitars and amplifiers, Jimi touched on a couple anecdotes. One time, he was being left at the roadside when touring in the U.S. as a session guitarist. Timekeeping was not one of his greatest skills, and after waiting a while, the band left him to make his own way to the next gig! I had the notion that although Jimi was aware of his impact on the music scene, he was never really bothered about the money aspect of his fame. He was happy as long as he had a couple of bucks in his pockets! In contrast, Noel was far more concerned with the finances, which apparently led to one or two arguments down the line. Apparently, it was Jimi's only time at Folkestone, and after the session he stayed with Noel at his mother's home in nearby Seabrook. The story goes, as the weather was very cold, Jimi wrote one of his hits, called "Fire", while staying at his bass guitarist's home that night. There was a memorable line, "Move over Rover, and let Jimi take over", Rover being the name of Noel's family dog! Oddly, although I had a jam alongside Jimi Hendrix, I never, ever saw him in a rock concert! Interestingly, I didn't realise the Jimi Hendrix Experience were rehearsing in the same Grace Hill venue the following day! Missed out on that one!

While Noel was carving out global fame with the Jimi Hendrix Experience, Hayley was still steaming ahead with various film projects. During 1965, she starred in "The Truth About Spring" alongside James MacArthur, experiencing her first screen kiss. Hayley followed this film with "The Trouble With Angels" in 1966, which proved to be a massive hit. The story revolved around a Catholic schoolgirl and the various scrapes she managed to get into. Every time she planned a prank, she used the catchphrase, "Scathingly brilliant idea", which always ended with her being in hot water! These two films were the first of the post Disney era for Hayley, but nevertheless, several films followed after "The Family Way". After completing "Pretty Polly" in 1967, Hayley joined Roy Boulting again, and indeed, Hywel Bennett, in the creepy thriller, "Twisted Nerve". The garden shed scene close to the end of the film was a piece of classic film direction. Very little evidence of obvious horror, but with a tangible emotional impact!

Another Boulting Brother production followed in 1971, "Mr Forbush and the Penguins", co-starring John Hurt. The film I enjoyed, however, apparently had disappointing receipts at the box office. This proved a busy year for Hayley, as she also married Roy Boulting, having worked with him on the "Family Way" film.

Back in 1961, when Hayley's elder sister, Juliet, married Russell. At the time, I was just a teen, who somehow imagined being totally in love with Juliet, which of course, was just plain daft! I had never even met her, certainly never spoken to her, and possibly shared my thoughts with countless other like-minded teens! By 1971, I was twenty six, a little more worldly-wise, and, more importantly, had experienced meeting with Hayley. It is a truth in life, we can meet people who we take an instant shine to, regardless of their sex or job or in Hayley's case her fame. As I previously mentioned, at that first meeting in Cowden, we never once touched on her films or fame. Just two teenagers hanging out in the sun, enjoying a few quiet moments. With Juliet, I felt the real sense of betrayal, although in my shallow teenage head, an emotion that evaporated incredibly swiftly! When I read in the newspapers that Hayley had married Roy Boulting, I felt genuinely pleased for her. Perhaps, I might have had a 'gosh' moment over their thirty three years age disparity, especially having had my sister marry a chap twice her age in 1968, which in turn proved to be a very short-lived union! But if a couple are in love, surely the age difference doesn't matter. With Hayley, even given that initial, relatively short conversation, I had read past the cover and discovered a person I could easily relate to in life. It was one of those once in a lifetime chance meetings where our paths had crossed. Hayley would continue her acting career in films and on the stage, and I would follow my dreams.

Indeed, by the time Hayley married Roy, I had sold a

successful crash repair garage in Folkestone, and bought a bungalow in Lyminge, called "Krakatoa", named after the famous volcano, close to Java, which violently erupted in the 1880's. The eruption was so devastating, nine square miles of land disappeared under the sea, creating one of the biggest tidal waves known to mankind! With the funds gained from the garage sale, I bought and ran a Pony Trekking Centre on the Romney Marsh in Kent, with twenty six ponies and horses! Sadly, Hayley's marriage to Roy finally ended in 1977, and my divorce with the horses was a year earlier in 1976, when the National Westminster Bank gently took me by the financial hand and said enough is enough! It was a dream, but I was totally out of my league! It is one thing to ride on a Sunday morning, but another suddenly being confronted by twenty six hungry mouths, especially in the winter months! It was a financial disaster, but the Peter Pan, which lurks in my cosmic spirit, came to my aid! It was not entirely the end of a dream. Having found homes for eleven of the horses, I moved the remaining fifteen to a new location in the glorious Kentish countryside at Everden, close to the village of Hawkinge, where, as mentioned before, was home to the famous Spitfire fighters, which during the war had defended our coastline from the Luftwaffe, against a possible German invasion! Included in the rental was not only the grazing field, but also the use of a very old stable block divided into loose boxes with cobbled floor and complete, with a hayloft above. The nearby bonus being a beautiful example of a Kentish Oast House! All this for five pounds a week, mind you, this was 1971! The huge bonus was, apart from the amazing network of bridleways that wound their way around the stunning woods and lanes of the Alkham Valley, I met a special rider who became the future Mrs. Wright!

After completing the film "Endless Sleep" in 1972, based

on the same name novel by Agatha Christie, and again co-starring Hywel Bennett, Hayley put her 'Pollyanna' image totally behind her after completing the Philip Levene adaptation of his own story, "Deadly Strangers", a rather dark drama where Hayley plays the part of a scheming psychopath! Personally, I thought it was a well constructed story with a real twist at the end!

At this time in her career, Hayley basically took a bit of time out from filming, especially as she and Roy had their first son, Crispian, in 1973. But before she did, Hayley explored her other skill of treading the boards in the footsteps of her father and sister. She had already gained experience in the theatre, with such West End productions as "Peter Pan" in 1966, and Noel Coward's "Suite in Two Keys", for which she won the Theatre World Award. She appeared in the delightful comedy "A Touch of Spring", performed at the Comedy Theatre in London in 1975. This play would prove to be a turning point for both her and me!

Although over the years, I faithfully followed Hayley's film life, watching the various productions in which she had starred, including cutting out the odd newspaper items which concerned her life. It was brilliant to read in one of the daily newspapers an advertisement concerning the forthcoming stage production of "A Touch of Spring" at the Comedy Theatre in Panton Street, Westminster, which has since been renamed 'The Harold Pinter Theatre' in 2011, to honour the memory of the playwright, who had died three years previously. Having given it some thought, I decided to see Hayley in this light-hearted romantic comedy. Obviously, I had seen most of her many films, but never seen her in a live production, and this was the opportunity. Besides, it would be a mini break to travel up to London for the day. I deliberately chose a midweek day, as the stables were busy at the weekend. Tina, the stable groom, was competent, so I knew the horses would be in safe hands. The train journey to London's Charing Cross was exciting. There was this memory of how I felt when I took the train to Tonbridge and hitched a lift to Cowden, several years previously. As I had plenty of time on my hands, and as an avid tea drinker, the first port of call was the famous Lyons Corner House, close to the Charing Cross terminus, and opposite Trafalgar Square. The Comedy Theatre in Panton Street was relatively a short walk from the Corner House, with the route taking me through the Square. The temptation to stop and feed the pigeons on the way was too great. Having purchased a bag of corn from the vendor, who seemed permanently covered with pigeons, I took up a position by one of the fountains. Interestingly enough, every pigeon in the square promptly decided they needed to be my friend! They landed on my head, on my shoulders, and on my hands! In the end, I found it expedient to drop the bag and walk swiftly away, although not before the birds had inadvertently bombed me! Fortunately, the birds lost interest in me after the food was gobbled up, and I managed to do a quick cleanup with the aid of the fountain water! It was a warm sunny day, plus with the short walk to the theatre, I arrived fairly spotless. Well, no-one stared or pointed at any rate!

To this day, I still find that one of the joys of live theatre is sitting in your seat before the show begins. Theatregoers full of anticipation, milling about looking for their seats, clutching their tickets and programmes in the semi-gloom of the house lights, which remain up to aid people to find their seat. This can be a nightmare if the light is too low, making the small alphabet badges on the end of each row almost impossible to see. Once seated, there is that glorious hubbub of noisy chatter, and of course the obligatory standing to allow people to pass to their seat! This is always a problem if you are sitting at the end of the row, as every person has to get by you! But eventually the house lights dip, a hush sweeps across the theatre, the fire curtain ascends, the curtain draws wide, and the music starts. The stage is set for the story to unfold! Live theatre is pure magic, as this show proved to be the case for both Hayley and me, for different reasons!

4 RENEWED BEGINNINGS

"A Touch of Spring" was a couple of hours well spent at the Comedy Theatre in 1975. The play, written by Samuel Taylor, appeared as a film production in 1972, as "Avanti", in which Hayley's sister, Juliet, starred. A stage production was also put on at the Yvonne Arnaud Theatre in Guildford in 1972, entitled "Friends, Romans and Lovers". In essence, this romantic comedy revolves around a married American businessman arriving in Italy to retrieve the body of his father, who was killed in a car accident. Faced with Italian red tape, he engages a young local male to help - at a cost. In the meantime, he meets and enters into an affair with a young woman, who turns out to be the daughter of his father's lover! It is an impossible situation, which is resolved by the American businessman and young woman replicating their respective parents' love affair, by promising to meet once a year, as their parents had done for the previous twelve years, in Rome. Hayley played 'Alison', the young woman. Leigh Lawson had the character of 'Baldassare Pantalone', and Peter Donat, the businessman. Also, in the cast was

Julian Fellowes, who was to have a huge success many years later as the writer of "Downton Abbey". Hayley did not appear at the start of the performance, but when she did make her entrance, a thunderous wall of appreciative applause came her way. The production had to pause for a few seconds until the applause abated and the play could continue! The whole production was flawless. The chemistry between the actors was brilliant, and of course, Hayley's performance was second to none, especially her sense of timing and delivery of dialogue. This all being confirmed by the sound of the rapturous applause at the end of the show, as the cast took their curtain call. I felt genuinely pleased for Hayley. She was married, she had her young son Crispian, a fantastic career behind her and, assuredly, in front of her. Life was looking positive.

During the return rail journey across the rolling Kentish countryside, I had the opportunity to reflect on the events of the day. It crossed my mind to write to her and congratulate her on the production. I didn't have her address, unlike the time at Cowden. All I knew, Hayley and Roy had plans to live in a converted early nineteenth century windmill, snuggled away in the Chiltern Hills, near Ibstone in Buckinghamshire. Much later on, I discovered this smock mill named Cobstone Mill, actually dates back to the sixteenth century, and was later rebuilt in 1816. It was historically referred to as the Turville Windmill, as it stands on Turville Hill, overlooking the nearby village of the same name.

The only address I had for Hayley was The Comedy Theatre in Panton Street, so yes, it made sense to try my luck and send a letter there. Of course, I never kept copies of letters sent to Hayley, so I had to rely on a forty-five-year-old memory to determine the contents of that initial correspondence! No doubt it would have alluded to the

Cowden wedding celebration of her sister Juliet in 1961, and the brief meeting on their family farm, later in 1963, where I found her hanging over a farm gate! I guess the letter would have touched on the production of "A Touch of Spring", expressing how much I enjoyed the entire production, complimenting her performance, especially as I had never seen her in a stage production. Tentatively, I remember putting my address on the top of the correspondence, with the understanding that I had a fifty-fifty chance of a reply, or perhaps even at best, I could expect a standard autographed photograph! Can you imagine my delight and surprise to receive a handwritten letter, dated 7th July 1975!

For a while, I sat just staring at the London postmarked envelope, before carefully opening it with a knife. As I was certain, whatever the contents were, it would be preserved in my memory souvenir box! Indeed, there was no autographed publicity photograph, but a handwritten letter from Hayley. Written as a postscript, the sentiment at the end of the letter has continued to resonate with me, down through the decades, and indeed is indicative of the warm and natural person Hayley is. It reads, and I quote, "Whatever you do, wherever you are, I do with you, good luck and much happiness". This was a justified "wow" moment in my life! All I remember was getting through two, possibly three, cups of tea, before carefully folding the letter and returning it to its envelope home! While sipping the tea, it gave me time to reflect on this wonderful new development, and to question my own intellectual and emotional motives. Seeing her dressed as the bridesmaid at Cowden, and being a typical besotted sixteen year old fan, teenage sexual fantasies fuelled it. The second time at Cowden, I had witnessed a glimpse of the person behind all the fame charade, and I much liked what I saw. What would the future hold? The honest answer and subsequent conclusion reached was exactly what Hayley had written to me! Whatever you do. Wherever you are, I do with you.

My first wife, who helped with the stables, had not long since galloped off into the sunset with her younger colt, so I guess there was a mixture of feeling vulnerable, plus a pinch of feeling sorry for myself, and backed up by a good dose of having a failure complex! Considering where I was emotionally, possibly I was reading too much into receiving the letter! However, friendship is to be treasured, and it appears we were both on the same page! A pang of reality, of course, swamped over me. This was pure conjecture on my part, since I was basing this assumption on one meeting made years previously, and one letter! The tangible point is the letter was handwritten, which indicated a personal touch. Perhaps it was the act of a person, who although enjoying incredible international success, perhaps reached out to encompass a simple degree of normality.

The letter from The Comedy Theatre went with the autographed photograph received back in 1964, into my memory box. Both my life and Hayley's were incredibly busy and traumatic during the early seventies. I previously mentioned, my first wife had galloped off!

The backdrop was that I had married a young woman from Folkestone in 1970, which proved fairly catastrophic, as it lasted just a couple of years. The garage that I had started with a £5.00 note in 1965, I sold early in 1971 for a healthy return. With the proceeds, I purchased the trekking centre in which I worked alongside my first wife, initially on the Romney Marsh in Kent, but later on the north Downs between Folkestone and Dover. Sadly, one of the clients became a tad more than a regular rider by trotting off into the sunset, with my wife. The consequence, by1974, I was back living on my own again, in our marital home "Krakatoa". Clearly, my ex-wife and her new partner proved to be a match made in heaven, as they eventually married and had a long life together. Clearly meant for each other. The merry-go-round that is life never fails to amaze me. About a year, or two later, there was a young woman who caught my eye. She was a regular Sunday trekker who would ride out with an old school friend, and after a while I found myself looking forward to the Sunday Trek. Being a bit slow in coming forward, it took until 1976 to finally invite the future Mrs Wright out to the pictures. We decided on the controversial western film "Soldier Blue". It was this film that dispelled the myth that the indigenous native Indians of North America were the bad guys. It was the invading white soldiers dressed in blue after all! The film depicted the true account of the appalling massacre of women and children on their reservation at Sandy Creek, Colorado Territory, by the U.S Cavalry in 1864, as a direct revenge for a previous battle with the Indian nation, resulting in the bluecoats sustaining heavy losses. The last twenty minutes of the film were visually, truly shocking. Personally, I was surprised by the degree of violence that managed to get past the watchful eye of the film censors. But then, sometimes, we need to be shocked out of our complacency to witness the savagery of war! Apart from the obvious violence, the language was rather ripe too! The worst culprit is the leading lady, Candice Bergen! Having played in rock bands, I was certainly no prude, having heard most things expletive, especially when the alcohol flowed! But I did remember, tut-tutting, apparently quite vociferously in the cinema as the expletives were hurled towards us from the silver screen! The future, rather bemused Mrs Wright, was sitting next to me on our first date, apparently thinking, "what the hell planet does this bloke live on?"

Hayley's life was going through a turbulent time in the seventies too. She and Roy Boultng had married in 1971, with Crispian their son arriving on 18th January 1973. Hayley juggled, being a young mum and also pursuing her professional career. She completed two films for Sidney Hayers, "What Changed Charley Farthing" in 1974, followed by "Deadly Strangers" in 1975. Just one more film followed shortly after, called "The Kingfisher Caper" based on the novel, "The Diamond Hunters", written by Wilbur Smith, with the screenplay by Roy Boulting and Lee Marcus. Around the time I was bombed with pigeon poo on the way to see "A Touch Of Spring", Hayley had more or less retired from the silver screen, but other events were to turn her life in a new direction. A few years previously, their youngest daughter had met her parents unusually early at Heathrow airport, to impart some important news. The three of them went to a cafe to have breakfast. Hayley was bubbling over with excitement and dying to let her parents know the news, which became apparent when she showed the engagement ring on her finger!

"Gosh! Who is the lucky fellow?" was, of course, the first question posed by her father.

"It's Roy, I am in love with him," Hayley replied, beaming from ear to ear. Her father had leaned forward to inspect the ring more closely, and unfortunately the stool he was perched on tilted over, resulting with him being unceremoniously dumped on the floor with his breakfast!

This comedic moment gave her father time to gather his thoughts and prepare his fatherly advice by pointing out that although Roy was suited to take his daughter's hand, especially as he was an articulate and successful director, the obviously large age difference could prove a problem. She might, at some point, meet and fall in love with a man nearer her age. It was evident that the prediction her dad had made was coming to pass. This is exactly what happened when performing with Leigh Lawson in "A Touch of Spring"!

Hayley and Roy split in 1974, and she moved in with Leigh in the late seventies, sharing a spacious house in South Norwood, where their son Jason was born. Leigh was an impeccable actor with many fine stage, film and television productions to his credit. Personally, two of my favourites were the television series "The Travelling Man" and his part in the Roman Polanski's film drama, "Tess of the d'Urbervilles". He also made a name for himself as stage director, with hits such as "If Love Were All", which opened at the Lucille Lortel Theatre, off Broadway in 1999, co-written by Leigh and Sheridan Morley.

My personal life was also moving on. As I previously mentioned, my future wife was a client at the trekking centre I was operating in the North Downs between Folkestone and Dover. It is probably true of most friendships, that it helps start having something in common. In this case, it was horses again! When you consider, much of our historical civilisation has been built on the backs of our equine friends, I suspect many friendships have been initiated by a shared love of horses. The horses gave me one of those rare magical moments, which last your entire lifetime, having occurred while running the Everden Stables, situated close to the scenic Alkham valley. Apart from the acreage I rented adjacent to the stable and outbuilding, I also had the use, granted by a local farmer, of an extensive rolling valley of some one hundred acres, situated some two or three hundred yards away, down the country lane from the stables. Most days when I collected them, the horses and ponies would be standing by the field gate, patiently waiting to be taken the short walk to the stable, and breakfast! This particular day they were not! On hopping over the gate, I could see them at the farthest point on the other side of the valley! I ran a little way down my side of the valley, calling. Immediately I saw fifteen heads shoot up, followed by the sound of sixty hooves thundering down the other side of the valley and up towards me. What a sight! Tails and manes flying! As they neared, I turned to run with them! For a few seconds, I was with them, indeed not just with them, but part of them, sharing the spirit of the moment! Then they were gone! I was just following the dust cloud, created by the galloping hooves, to the field gate, where they were stomping and snorting in their excitement, and of course, waiting for their amble along the short distance to their breakfast. A magical moment indeed!

Horses prominently featured in the life of my future father-in-law, during World War Two, when he was captured at Dunkirk in 1940, having been told to defend a road leading into the town. He was a corporal in charge of six soldiers, with a rifle each and a few sandbags. After a while, a German tank division rumbled down the road towards them. No shots were fired, as it was a hopeless situation! The convoy stopped, and a German officer alighted from the leading tank and strode over to the defenders. He explained very succinctly in perfect English. The choices were extremely limited, surrender or suffer the consequences! My future father-in-law said the only noise to be heard, apart from the rumble of the tank engines, was the sound of seven rifles being dropped on the road! They were all in the bag! Life at first was not bad. He and one other were put on a German farm and worked the fields. However, it was always considered a duty to attempt an escape! This they did in an audacious manner. They nicked a horse from the farm, and riding by the cover of darkness and holding up during the day, they managed to dodge German Patrols before finally reaching Rotterdam in Holland, where they hoped somehow, to pinch a boat and get back to Blighty! They got caught and sent back to the security of a prison camp in the Black Forest, where various other adventures befell them, before being finally released by the American troops in 1945.

5 WE TIE THE KNOT AND SHARE CHAMPERS WITH HAYLEY

Having received Hayley's letter, and not content with seeing her in "A Touch of Spring" just once, I decided to revisit The Comedy Theatre and watch the production again in 1976. It was just as great the second time round. Thoroughly enjoyable! On my return, I wrote again to the theatre, mainly because I was unaware Hayley was planning to move to Norwood. When the reply came, her letter not only included her new home address, which totally bowled me over, as it showed a degree of trust regarding her privacy, but also offered again the chance to come backstage and chat!

I missed the production of Daphne du Maurier's timeless classic, "Rebecca," which Hayley had starred in 1977. She had very kindly written a letter inviting me to the show and come backstage afterwards, but unfortunately with my workload at the time, it proved impossible. However, I was given the opportunity to catch her, playing at the Churchill Theatre in Bromley in March 1978, alongside Ian Lavender, who had found fame for his hilarious portrayal of Private

Pike in "Dad's Army". This was a comedy entitled "My Fat Friend" written by Charles Laurence. The show was hilarious, and I was so excited at the prospect of going backstage afterwards, something I had never done before. After the show, I left the theatre and had walked around the building. I found the rear stage entrance, and, would you believe it, I blew it! I was totally unnerved by the large gathering of people at the stage door, many of whom clutched autograph books! The thought of pushing through the crowd and then being confronted by a doorman, whose response to my request to visit Miss Mills might have been met with "in your dreams mate!," was too daunting to me!

My response was to shuffle, with my spirits and my head hung low, off into the night to seek refuge in my car. There was time to ponder the stage door event during my drive back across Kent, towards Folkestone, and it highlighted a flaw in my emotional makeup! I was confident enough to stand on any stage, playing rock music, but painfully shy offstage. I felt uncomfortable with any big drinking events after the show, where people with too much alcohol would lose the plot! I much preferred stopping off on the way home with the other band members, together with our respective girlfriends, for a late-night chat around a dining table in an all-night cafe, like 'The Oasis', which was one of my favourite, and aptly named, given its location as being on a remote part of the Romney Marshes in Kent.

Having left the Bromley theatre behind, it occurred to me that part, and parcel of Hayley's fame, as with all celebrities, is the army of adoring fans, who seek that prized autograph, or perhaps a handshake. I had actually crossed over into Hayley's professional world. I decided to take the view that if Hayley had invited me backstage that evening, perhaps those waiting outside might never have seen her! How selfish of me that would have been! At least, that is what I told myself to convince myself I was not just being a feeble wimp!

If I had gone backstage, part of our conversation would include my exciting news that I had become engaged with the wedding planned for later in October the same year. A few days later, I wrote to Hayley offering my feeble excuses for not fighting my way through the crowd at the stage door, but also announcing the forthcoming marriage.

It was a while before receiving a reply, which genuinely led me to believe perhaps I had blown it, but no, an amazing reply came, which totally overlooked my idiosyncrasies. It was an invitation to her home in Norwood to share a bottle of Champagne, close to our wedding date in October!

Apparently, Leigh would not be there, as he would be on location in France for the 1978 Polanski production of "Tess of the d'Urbervilles". Obviously, I wrote back accepting Hayley's generous offer, and her impeccable timing. Our planned honeymoon in Essex was not a million miles from Hayley's London home.

Our wedding day, towards the end of October 1978, was beautiful. And considering the lateness of the season, the weather was incredibly kind to us and the guests! We had married in Folkestone's registry office where we garnered a mild rebuke from the usher, as far too many guests had arrived. I must say it was packed, with standing room only! It was so tempting to reply to the stern-faced usher, that I promised never to repeat this breach of rules again, but good counsel in my head dictated I refrained from any such remark! After the ceremony, we all strolled across the road in the autumnal sunshine to enter the picturesque, ornamental Kingsnorth Gardens, which attracts thousands of tourists, to have our wedding photographs taken. These gardens were originally part of a brick works, so effectively, a quarry, which eventually became abandoned by the late nineteen-twenties, and descended into a series of allotments and rubbish tips! Interestingly, it had apparently belonged to my great, great, grandmother, back in the Victorian era. The story goes she was a great poker player, but maybe not so great, as she gambled it away during one session! It ended up in the hands of a certain John Kingsnorth, and eventually, after various negotiations, Folkestone Town Council took over the site and developed it into the present day magnificent gardens, which opened in 1928.

After the wedding photograph session, we all adjourned to the Swingfield Village Hall, a few miles away, amongst the glorious rolling downs, for the wedding breakfast and a knees up! What a brilliant day everyone had. Life was looking good. Here I was, married to the girl of my dreams, having just bought a wonderful old 1814 farmhouse, set in a couple of acres, on the outskirts of Lyminge, in the heart of the Kentish countryside. Skeete Place, for us, was a piece of idyllic heaven, partially hidden down a country lane that morphed into a bridle path. The gardens were a mass of fruit trees, including apple, pear, plum, and cherry with intermittent rose beds, and all surrounded by a wall of May trees which bloomed their white blossoms brilliantly every spring. My transport business, which had risen Phoenix style from the ashes of my disastrous equestrian dreams, was doing well. To cap it all, we had a honeymoon in Essex to look forward to, followed by a trip to Hayley's home in Norwood. However, in reality, work commitments for both my wife and me dictated it would be a short break! My other half was P.A in a busy pharmaceutical firm, whilst the transport business was hotting up for the Christmas rush. A fair amount of my trade came through the nearby Dover Docks, where, not surprisingly, the greatest traffic was the wine imports!

After spending a long weekend in Essex, we drove back

around the infamous M25, lovingly nicknamed the biggest car park in the UK, and headed for South Norwood, situated on the west side of London. Hayley and Leigh's home was not difficult to find, being located on the edge of a large green, where parking was not an issue. Mounting the steps to the front door, I suddenly felt a little nervous, remembering the last time I had actually seen Hayley was in the play, "My Fat Friend", resulting in me skulking off into the night rather than pushing through the crowds. The door swung open, and we were both greeted with a peck on the cheek and a hug from a beaming Hayley. Having relieved us of our coats, she led us through to her lounge, where we were invited to sit and make ourselves comfortable. The conversation flowed straight away, the subject mainly being the events of the wedding day and the new home in Kent. At some point in the proceedings, I managed to mumble a word of apology with reference to the Bromley fiasco, which was graciously dismissed with a grin and a wave of her hand. After a short while, between conversational anecdotes, Hayley disappeared and returned clutching a bottle of bubbly, and some nibbles. She handed me the bottle to open, and as usual, the "Jonah" lurking in the shade of my psychic consciousness took control, and the cork refused to budge! Of course, I was terrified of hitting either my wife or Hayley with the flying cork, or indeed sending a tidal wave of champagne over the carpet! After a few moments of terror, Hayley took the bottle back off me and nimbly flicked the cork, which immediately released itself! After toasting us on our future marriage, we sat and engaged in a conversation ranging from babies and families to life in general. Hayley apologised for Leigh not being there, but he was still engrossed in portraying the character of the evil villain, 'Alec', in the sad Thomas Hardy story of "Tess of the d'Urbervilles',' where the tormented Tess is hanged for killing her wretched antagonist. The film was shot on location in France, as the director, Roman Polanski, had legal issues filming in the UK. After a few pleasant hours, it was time to take our leave. Hayley showed us to the door, gave us a hug, and waved us off into the gloom of the encroaching evening. Obviously, we both wanted to chat about the visit, but this was pre-satellite navigation, and we were initially engaged in working out the return journey, rather than getting lost up some cul-de-sac! After finally meeting with the M25 again and the subsidiary A20, which heads towards Folkestone, the conversation finally turned towards our visit. We both agreed that Hayley, was engaging and incredibly friendly as the hostess, and also a good conversationalist, especially as I can natter on for the world! I have noticed Hayley always deliberates before making a reply. She absorbs information, reflects and delivers a relevant response. This is certainly true in interviews. The conversation had tended to veer away from the entertainment industry, or indeed, about acting in general. The nearest reference concerned Leigh, working in France. The day had been more about accepting the hospitality from a charming person, who genuinely wanted to meet us, and be regaled with our wedding anecdotes! Interestingly enough, all these years on, we still don't mention much about her career, or mine for that matter! I believe it goes back to that first meeting in Cowden, where no mention was made about the famous films she had made, or for that matter, her celebrity status at that point. Perhaps she felt comfortable in the company of people talking to Hayley the person, as opposed to Hayley the International Star! In all the years I have known her, I have never once asked her for a photograph, which probably proves the point! This was brought up in conversation a few years ago, just before the pandemic, where Hayley said we ought to remedy the situation. I look forward to that time.

6 WORK AND BABIES

By the time we visited Hayley's home in South Norwood to crack open the bottle of champagne, she would have had her hands full with two young sons to care for, especially Jason, who was born in January 1976, the result of the love affair that had developed between Hayley, and Leigh Lawson, her leading man in "A Touch of Spring". Leigh was prolific on the acting front, especially filming. Prior to making "Tess of the D'urbervilles", he was contracted to portray the character of James Black aka Giacomo Nerone in the 1977 film, which was based on the novel written by Morris West, called "The Devil's Advocate". A wartime storyline, full of intrigue, set in Catholic Italy. One of Leigh's co-stars was Hayley's dad, John Mills! Interestingly enough, it was mainly filmed in Germany. In the meantime, Hayley would be at home looking after the two young lads, and juggling with the play "My Fat Friend" in 1978. It must have been an emotional time for both Hayley and Leigh, as she was only recently divorced from her husband Roy Boulting, and Leigh had also just divorced from his first wife, Mondy. Like any young mother, Hayley took a step back and concentrated on her young family. However, in 1981, she was offered a leading part in a seven part television serial called "The FlameTrees of Thika", based on a novel by Elspeth Huxley and adapted by John Hawkesworth for the small screen. This story is set in Kenya, just before the First World War, and proved to be a renaissance for Hayley's career. The series was an incredible success and was duly nominated for three BAFTA awards, including Ian Wilson winning best cinematography for his work.

Interestingly, this was a really uplifting time for Hayley, and by now we were corresponding on a regular basis. As a result, towards the end of 1981, I was able to let Hayley and Leigh know we were expecting a baby! The doctor told us in 1979, we could not have children, due to a dramatic horse riding accident my wife had endured! The accident occurred whilst my wife reached over to undo a field gate, whilst still mounted, which is a normal manoeuvre in riding. However, on that particular day, the wind was blowing a hooly, with the result 'Fraser' without warning, shied away from the gate. Unfortunately, as she gripped the gate, this unexpected movement yanked her out of the saddle and dumped her on her back, between the gate and the horse. Sadly, this spooked him further, and he proceeded to dance across my wife! One of his hind hooves landed on her thigh, but mercifully did little damage, as the ground was, thankfully, wet and very muddy, resulting in her being pushed into the mire. Sadly, the other hind caught her a glancing blow between her legs. Bearing in mind, Fraser was wearing metal shoes and weighed about 500 kilograms. It was a serious accident, with serious consequences. Having said that, my wife displayed the true colours of a horse lover, even being in intense pain whilst being carted off to hospital. She still managed to yell: "Is Frazer alright?"

After leaving the hospital, my wife had to recuperate for twelve months and learn how to deal with a totally irregular menstrual cycle, and the notion that the probability of ever carrying a baby was remote! When we had married in 1978, we had already decided not to have a child, as we enjoyed our lifestyle with the horses and our lovely old house set amongst the picturesque countryside. Life was good! It is a strange phenomenon. The moment someone says you cannot have something, you immediately have this sense of longing for the impossible. This was an incredibly difficult period for my wife, being just twenty nine at the time. This, however, was to dramatically change in 1981, when, having abandoned any contraceptive aid as it seemed pointless, my wife announced one morning she felt very 'strange'! Not a bad 'strange', but an interesting, first time 'strange'! I believe we mentioned various possibilities, ranging from drinking perhaps a tad too much alcohol the previous evening to possibly too much exercise! Eventually, we got talking about the possibility of being pregnant, although we both agreed to rule out that option. Nevertheless, my wife deemed fit to run upstairs, where she kept a few pregnancy testing kits. My wife worked as a PA for a pharmaceutical company, which produced the said kits and allowed staff to have samples of their various toiletries. Imagine our surprise and rejoicing when the dark ring started to form in the specimen! We decided to get our findings verified before we hit the family and friends with this extraordinary, but exciting news! We had a very interesting dialogue with the local doctor, who had monitored my wife through the whole episode since the accident, especially at the point he mentioned he was convinced he would get her pregnant eventually! The family was over the moon for us, as were indeed our friends. Among the letters of congratulations was one from Hayley, which carried so much generous sentiment, as she knew of the situation from the word go! As with all the other letters, I have kept them to this day!

Joe was born twenty fifth of May 1982. What a great day!

Apart from the success and awards "The Flame Trees of Thika" bought her, Hayley found her diary busy with theatre work. The last role I had seen Hayley in was in 1978, in the renowned Oscar Wilde comedy, "The Importance of Being Earnest", playing the part of 'Gwendoline'. We had travelled down to Chichester, to the famous Festival Hall there, and subsequently stayed overnight. It was a unique experience, as the theatre is in the round. The audience basically surrounds the cast on a low lying centre stage. The acting technique has to alter to cater for this layout. In many ways, a far more natural way of acting is to reflect normal life. The original London Globe theatre, built in 1599, is a good example of how the early actors had shaped their craft acting in the round. Oddly enough, many years later, when performing with a northern band named CA9, we had one such experience playing in the round, at a venue just on the outskirts of Gateshead. Although our amps were mic'd up to the house quadraphonic sound system, I found it a trifle confusing, to keep turning around to face the audience, which surrounded the band! Even more difficult for our drummer, John Alderson, he had no choice which way he faced!

After the Chichester show, we met with Hayley at the Festival Hall, where we had a chat and a quick drink, before retiring to a local hotel for the night. As previously mentioned, our son Joe was born 25th May 1982. Two days later, Hayley opened in a drama called "Talley's Folly", written by Lansford Wilson, at the Lyric Theatre in Hammersmith, London. On some opening nights, I would send Hayley a bouquet of flowers, as I did on this occasion, especially as it was so close to the birth of our Joe, and all the celebrating that goes with the event. Hayley sent back an absolutely charming letter of congratulations to the three of us. Joe's mother was a generous person in many ways, and after a couple of weeks, suggested I take time off and go to see Hayley at the Lyric. Possibly, there was an ulterior motive, as the two grandmothers were in constant attendance and I was getting under everyone's feet! It was a great play. Not the normal comedy, but a serious drama, set by the Missouri River in an old boathouse attached to a farm where 'Talley' lived. Hence the title "Talley's Folly". Apart from the superb acting performance of Hayley, and her co-star Jonathan Pryce, both delivered a highly charged and passionate filled dialogue. Given there were only two characters, and no intermission, three other things stood out in my mind. Firstly, the set itself is complete with a river bank and river, plus a row boat moored alongside! Secondly, a full moon, which rose from stage left and waned, after following an arc to stage right during the two hour drama! And, thirdly, a bit of theatre that did not work! The idea was novel, but in execution it simply wasn't going to happen! When first entering the auditorium, the lights are up, allowing the excited audience, full of their sometimes noisy vocal anticipation, to find their seats. Of course, they are always accompanied by the rustling of their programmes, which list the storyline and information relating to two much loved British actors. My seat was third row back in the front stalls, so I would enjoy a first class view of the stage and the action. While the lights were still up, I noticed Jonathan Pryce, in his 1940's costume, enter from the rear of the auditorium and work his way down to the front of the stage and lean against it. The idea was for him to set the scene of the drama with some narrative. Of course, apart from a few rows close to him, no-one realised the play had commenced. There was just too much ambient audience noise! The inevitable then happened, with a growing sound of "shoosh" gradually radiating further outwards and backwards, like a Mexican wave, the auditorium then fell silent! In hindsight, it might have been better to dim the lights to gather the audience's attention, and then raise the lights for Jonathan to deliver his soliloquy! Funny enough, I went back a second time to see the play and couldn't help but notice the narration had been removed, with the drama commencing with the direct entrance of the two characters! After the second visit to the show, I caught up with Hayley backstage. The conversation tended to centre around young children and babies! I guess people's lives tend to fit the pattern. You go to school, then to work, get married, have a baby or two, with most of your contemporaries following the same line of thought! It was much the same with Hayley. Having said that, it was a source of great pleasure when she took me on the boards of the Lyric stage. Not many people can say they trod the stage of several well-known theatres across our fair land, even though just as a guest! One of the other perks is that you occasionally bump into fellow cast members, but alas, it was not to be this time, which was a shame, as I rate Jonathan Pryce as a great actor.

7 HEARTACHE

By late 1983, Hayley was still living in London, and we were still in the same old farm house on the outskirts of Lyminge in Kent. Although we kept in regular touch by letter, obviously visits were infrequent due to the distance, but I did make the effort to support Hayley by meeting up with her after a theatre show where possible. My transport business had taken off, especially after the Falklands war, when I landed a contract to deliver hundreds of new seating to the ferries that had been acquiesced by the military to transport military personnel and equipment to the South Atlantic. Life was all good! Wonderful baby boy, brilliant marriage to my life-partner, smashing horses, Fraser and Sultan, nibbling grass in the paddock in our rural retreat. Unfortunately for Hayley, her relationship with Leigh started to wane. At the time in January 1984, I had booked a ticket at the Vaudeville Theatre on the London Strand, to see her in a production of the famous detective story "Dial M for Murder" written by Frederick Knott,. Hayley's private life was making the news. It is a testament to her tenacity and sheer professionalism, that she was able to still give a first class performance. Having caught the early train to London, it was possible to attend the matinee, and catch up with Hayley for a while before she had to prepare for the evening performance. No mention of the newspaper story concerning the breakup was mentioned. She was more interested in how baby Joe was progressing, which again says a lot about the lady! Equally, I enquired after both Crispian and Jason. At one point, Simon Ward, her co-star in the play, knocked on her dressing room door and engaged her in some technical detail concerning the performance. I was given a quick, courteous and cordial introduction before he swiftly disappeared. The last time I had seen his face was in the film "Deadly Strangers", made in 1975, again starring alongside Hayley, in a brilliant psychological drama written by Philip Levene, and of course his portrayal of Winston Churchill in the film "Young Winston" had bought him much critical acclaim. Funnily enough, his co-star was none other than Hayley's father John Mills, with the director being Richard Attenborough.

Although we had mainly talked about babies and family, I sensed all was not well in the Hayley camp. I wanted to give her a big hug, but thought an emotional hug might destroy her mindset for doing another performance in a relatively short time. She was very much in my thoughts on my return to Charing Cross Railway station, at the end of the Strand. Hayley's situation remained with me as we crossed the Kentish countryside, until suddenly I realised the train was braking to arrive into Folkestone Central. As I climbed into my car and steered the bonnet towards Lyminge in the evening gloom, I felt compelled to revisit the Vaudeville Theatre and be more supportive, after all, that's what friends do! It was so good to get home to our small family bubble. Joe was in bed of course, but his mum had prepared a wonderful meal, which was much appreciated and heartily eaten, especially being accompanied by a glass of red wine! Being a lousy cook, we had come to a kitchen arrangement early in our relationship, whereby it was eminently sensible for Joe's mum to cook and me to do the washing up! We chatted about Hayley's personal problems concerning Leigh. We both agreed, it is one thing to have a problem within a relationship when neither are well known, but quite another situation when living your life in the glare of the paparazzi. It must be a nightmare! I suggested I return to London and revisit the Vaudeville Theatre after a week or so, just in a supportive role, and my wife agreed. Two weeks later, I found myself again staring at the Kentish countryside, as it flashed by on my way to London. It always reminds me of watching a movie with life rushing by! Again, I had booked a matinee ticket for "Dial M for Murder". Out of courtesy, I always checked out with Hayley to make sure it was okay to visit between the two performances. I actually had not heard from her, so I headed towards the theatre's booking office with a little trepidation. Eventually, I got to the head of the queue. Offered my name to the ticket clerk.

"Trevor Wright, do you say?"

"Well, someone has to be!" I quipped with a cheeky grin. Well, we were in a theatre!

"This was left for you", she replied with a smile as she pushed a small envelope towards me, with my name handwritten on the front. Instantly I recognised Hayley's writing. It was indeed an invite to go backstage between performances. The drama was just as impeccable the second time around as the first visit. The friendly chap on the stage door recognised me and greeted me with a big smile and asked,

"You visiting Miss Mills again? She did say you were coming and to give her a buzz", which he did. A few moments later, Hayley was at the stage door, and after a quick hug, I followed her through the labyrinth of the Vaudeville Theatre corridors, passing Peter Adamson on the way, who had famously played 'Len Fairclough' for many years in 'Coronation Street'. When we reached her dressing room, I noticed a bottle of wine and a couple of glasses waiting to be filled! We chatted about her situation. The conversation was private. By then, the breakup between Hayley and Leigh was making the national press. Leigh ended up dating and marrying the sixties model, Lesley Hornby, better known as 'Twiggy'. She and Leigh subsequently married in New York in 1988, and have remained married ever since. After about three quarters of an hour, Hayley intimated that there was a need to prepare for the evening performance. Of course, I had a pressing appointment with a train, which was hopefully sitting in Charing Cross. We retraced our footsteps to the stage doors. After a quick hug, I opened the door to leave, and immediately shut it again with great gusto on sighting hoards of press waiting outside! In that split second, I had experienced a glimpse of the downside of fame, and the invasion of privacy it brings! This was a totally alien world to me. The nearest I ever got to celebrity status was on one occasion in the sixties, when I had a cream tea with my Mum and Pop at their favourite Lathe Barn on the Romney Marsh. Now how rock'n'roll is that! Suddenly, our table was 'besieged' with three girls after my autograph!!! They had been at a Folkestone gig the previous night, where I was performing with The Mixed Feelings, and actually recognised me! Usually it is the vocalist or lead guitarist who becomes the focus of attention, not the bass guitarist! Mum and Pop were mildly amused or, rather bemused, as the three young ladies pushed bits of paper under my nose to sign!

"You did the right thing Trevor," Hayley said reassuringly

"I did?"

"Oh yes, your face might well have been splashed over the national press by the morning, inquiring who was the new man in my life!". There was a short pause before she continued, "Come on, I have another plan."

I followed her back through the theatre stalls to the entrance on the Strand. Apart from normal shoppers and commuters, there was no-one hovering by the Vaudeville, especially any paparazzi. We had another quick hug and peck on the cheek, and she disappeared back into the shadows of the theatre for her evening performance, whilst I ambled back towards the train that awaited me at Charing Cross. Once ensconced in my carriage, I could mull over the personal situation Hayley was in. When you are in the public eye, the press will follow you doggedly. Of course, it is essential to have the press on your side, especially for promotional publicity material. When I started the transport business, I soon realised the world was not waiting for T.I.Wright Transport to emerge. There had to be a marketing strategy. In consequence, a lot of time was spent on getting my name in the public domain, and more importantly, the quality of the service being offered. Perhaps that is the problem with celebrity culture. I dealt with inanimate objects, such as vans and lorries, that carried mass manufactured products. However, with celebrity status, the person becomes the product, which can overlook the fact that a celebrity is a normal human being with normal emotions. Since the fifties and the sixties, I had noticed a shift in the way publicity surrounded the new rock'n'roll era and the ever-growing film industry. It was very much controlled by management, with vetted press releases. There was an air of mystery regarding the celebrities, especially the pop artists. Based on my own experience as the local support band for The Who, on a couple of occasions, the management took full control of our sound system, to ensure their top line act had total impact when the curtains opened. This also raised another interesting insight into how the promotional side of entertainment worked. In those days, the curtains would be drawn shut to encapsulate that sense of mystery concerning the artist. This was clearly demonstrated on one occasion backing The Who, a band that I considered one of the world's finest rock bands. We had finished our stint as the warmup act, with the curtains closing to a rapturous applause from the audience, primarily not as a response to our set, but rather more an indication The Who, were about to appear! Roger, Pete, John and Keith were standing in the wings having a quick can or three! Their sound guys were making adjustments to the massive stack amplifiers. Just at that point, a voice of one of their management team came over the hall's P.A system, offering apologies to the massively excited crowd not to worry. The Who had been delayed due to traffic problems, but rest assured they would be performing, certainly within the next twenty to thirty minutes! They were already standing behind the stage curtains! They knew exactly what they were doing! When the curtains finally opened, it was absolute bedlam with the screaming and hysteria! But that is how it was. The curtains would open, the audience would have a glimpse of their favourite for an hour or so, and then whoosh! The curtains close and they are gone! The same applies to actors, and indeed most other entertainers. This stimulates interest in the performer, where the fan base wants more information about their particular hero. Of course, the paparazzi are only too happy to oblige, as the earnings can be quite astronomical! The never-ending circuit! The chicken and egg conundrum!

Hayley too, would have been subject to this media public frenzy. Her fan base globally, in the heady Disney days, exceeded even The Beatles. She had been dubbed the new Shirley Temple, the child actress from the thirties' era. There was a massive media interest in her. None more so, than when she had to make the transition from child to adult actor. Representing Hayley's best interests, her parents had already decided the film offer to star in "Lolita" was not an appropriate film or time in 1962, even though she would have worked alongside some greats of the screen, such as James Mason, Peter Sellers, plus being directed by the legendary Stanley Kubrick. The film content matter was in direct opposition to the "Pollyanna" image the Disney films had created. In the event, Sue Lyons took the role and won a Golden Globe award for her portrayal of "Lolita". However, I believe it was the right decision for their daughter. The way some Hayley's fans reacted when she did the brief nude, backside shot in the 1966 film "The Family Way" indicated the furore avoided by not being involved with the film "Lolita"!

I kept in touch with Hayley, in a supportive role, throughout this emotionally difficult period in her life. However, in one of her earlier letters of 1983, Hayley related some positive news. Since the huge hit with "The Flame Trees of Thika" she had no shortage of acting opportunities coming her way. Consequently during 1983 Hayley had accepted the role of Liz Walford in the evergreen play, "The Secretary Bird", by William Douglas Home. It was favourably reviewed at the Yvonne Arnaud Theatre, Guildford, before going into London. Having travelled to Guildford to see the play, one scene would be imprinted on my memory forever, and a day! The action for the play was set over two days, a Saturday and Sunday. The stage scene was a splendid country house, which included a Sunday morning breakfast feast. A long table full of various breakfast food plus mountains of crockery. The cast had just commenced their dialogue when a prop catastrophe struck! One of the table legs suddenly collapsed! The bowls, plates, cutlery, all went flying over the stage, as did the food and milk - it was total carnage! The audience collapsed into hysteria, as did the cast! Members of the stage crew, plus the cast, did what they could with the dilemma. They managed to make it look reasonable. The cast settled down and recommenced their dialogue to the point where, on cue, Gerald Harper playing the character Hugh Walford, makes an entrance. Gerald Harper stopped short when he spied the tidied-up mess and could not resist uttering the line: "I suppose breakfast is off!" Well, that was it again, the audience fell apart from laughing, as did the cast again! Probably not what William Douglas Home had in his mind when writing the play! The play was a romantic comedy, so it did not interfere with the evening. However, it could have ruined a serious play, as I witnessed once in the sixties. The Folkestone Repertory Company, run by Arthur Brough and later by Charles Vance, was housed in the beautiful Edwardian Leas Pavilion, situated on the famous cliff top walk in the centre of the town, where you might have seen H.G.Wells in a previous century, strolling along in deep thought, constructing in his head his futuristic novel, "The Time Machine". The play I watched was the old Victorian thriller "Gaslight" written by Patrick Hamilton. Not sure how or why it happened, but one actor had 'stitched-up' a fellow thespian! The result was that at the end of one dramatic scene, the victim took his Victorian frock coat from the hanger and began to put it on, but sadly found his sleeve had been stitched up! The poor chap desperately tried to keep his cool as he circled on the spot, in the vain hope of actually pushing his arms into the sleeves! The end came when the audience heard this great ripping sound, as the sleeve finally gave into the young actor's arm power, and he could then execute his exit! Another classic theatre anecdote at the same theatre was the occasion of having settled into our seats to enjoy a good drama. A voice came over the theatre PA system to announce that the leading man was unfortunately indisposed and would be replaced. We didn't give it much thought, these things happen. The curtains opened to a drawing room scene, with several library bookshelves lining the walls. An actor was positioned up a ladder studying a book he had pulled from the shelf, but curiously he was reading from a buff coloured booklet too. Seconds later, an actress entered the room, reading aloud from a similar buff book directed at the man still precariously perched on the ladder. Intriguingly, neither were looking at each other! A third actor joined them, and yes you guessed, he too, was reading his lines from a buff coloured book! To the audience's relief, the chap up the ladder left his lofty position and exited the room. The two remaining characters had to cuddle and embrace each other by having an arm around each other's head to continue reading the script! Then came the classic, side-splitting words "And the phone now rings", which it did, totally on cue! Needless to say, the theatre just collapsed into hysterics! It transpired, two members of the cast were indisposed, so as old adage decrees, the show must go on! The poor chap on the ladder was, in fact, the stage lighting engineer, and it was a question of, if you can read, get up that ladder!

On one occasion in the late nineties, I had experienced the nightmarish situation of being stuck on a stage totally on my own after my fellow thespian failed to appear on cue! Fortunately, it was Cinderella, the pantomime where the odd faux pas adds to the comedy. My character was Baron Hardup, father of Cinders. After some dialogue in the kitchen scene, Cinders leaves the kitchen via the door stage right. At this point, I exclaim in a extremely loud voice, "I am still the boss in my castle!" Whereon my 'wife' was supposed to appear at the door, rear stage, slap me round the face and cry out those immortal words 'Oh, no you're not!' Nothing happened! When I repeated the line, the audience sensed something had gone awry and loved it! I edged my way back to the rear of the stage, where I could see the director in the wings, waving his arms about in a demented fashion, shouting "Where's bloody Joan!" All I could think of was to improvise by taking the audience on a guided tour of my non-existent castle! Suddenly 'Joan' was bundled back on the stage, slapped me round the face with great force, whereupon I repeated my line "I am still the boss of my castle" at which my 'wife' slapped me around the face for a second time! The audience fell into hysterics!

After "The Secretary Bird" comedy, Hayley was offered, and accepted, a serious role in 1985 playing the character 'Carrie', in the Lillian Hellman play, "Toys in the Attic", at the Palace Theatre in Watford. Interestingly, Hayley's dad, Sir John Mills, was the President of the theatre at the time. Lillian Hellman was an accomplished playwright with quite a history. Born in New Orleans in 1905, she got caught up fighting against the Fascists during the Spanish Civil War in the thirties, and later helped the Russians to victory in World War Two. During this period she wrote some of her most successful plays, including "The Children's Hour" in 1934, followed by "The Little Foxes" in 1938, and "The Watch On the Rhine" in 1944. "Toys in the Attic" was written in 1960, and possibly her most successful play. Eager to see Hayley in a more serious drama, I had driven up to Watford to attend the performance and met up with Hayley afterwards. True to form, she had turned in a highly professional performance, alongside a brilliant cast including Helen Ryan, Gwen Watford, Doyle Richmond and Lysette Anthony, who was known for her role 'Lyssa' in the film "Krull".

Hayley seemed to be in a far better place now, and even shared an amusing anecdote which had happened to her on the first night of the play. The opening scene had Hayley on her hands and knees, brushing the drawing room carpet. She said fortunately she had her back to the audience, otherwise she would have got a fit of the giggles. Of course, as we all know, once that starts, there is very little wiggle room to get a straight face again! Apparently, there were two women sitting in the front stalls, making loud comments:

"Aye, you can tell she's never swept a carpet in her life!"

"You're right there Flo!" her friend chipped in, nodding with approval!

Hayley was upbeat, especially regaling me with this sweeping anecdote! By now, Leigh had moved on, and was an item with Twiggy, and Hayley had formed a friendship with her brother-in-law, Marcus Maclaine. He was the brother of Maxwell Caufield, who had married Juliet in 1980. They co-authored a book published in 1988 called "My God", with the proceeds going to 'Save The Children' Between them, Hayley and Marcus had sounded out a lot of celebrity friends to get their insight into a vision of the afterlife. It made excellent reading, with some serious comments coupled with some humorous anecdotes. Michael Winner came up with the super observation:

"Heaven must be compared to a wonderful tea party, complete with a selection of exceedingly good cakes!"

Life for the Wrights in our old farmhouse in Kent happily progressed through the eighties, made more complete by Joe's arrival in 1982. It was an idyllic place for a youngster to grow up. The garden stretched to 1.79 acres, with various fruit trees, including apple, plum, cherry and my favourite, a beautiful pear tree, which gave us this magnificent display of orange blossom regularly every spring. Besides this, a huge dense mass of raspberry bushes had taken over the middle of the garden. My street cred soared with Joe, when he was a little older. I would plonk him in a wheelbarrow and wheel him through a maze of pathways that I had hacked through the massive bush! Needless to say, many raspberries would disappear during the ride! We had also linked the two small grazing paddocks with what we called 'The Wibbly, Wobbly Way', which ran down the boundary fence with the neighbouring farmer. The path was designed to weave between the old established May trees. As with the pear tree, these mighty trees produced a stunning spring vista of white blossom. What a place for children to play! It had an 18 metre-long workshop tucked away in some trees and a stable block, consisting of four loose boxes, close to the entrance. We had many, happy family parties in this secluded piece of Kent. My parents and my two sisters with their families, and my wife's mum and brother.

Sadly, Joe never met his grandfather on his mother's side, as he passed away a year before Joe was born. Although he could be fierce on occasions, I had a lot of respect for him, particularly when relating his infamous wartime exploits, particularly his Dunkirk, and prisoner of war anecdotes! After his Dunkirk escapade, which ended with his capture at Rotterdam, he was subsequently incarcerated in a P.O.W. camp, deep in the Black Forest. Life here was certainly no walk in the park! After a few months, he and a fellow prisoner decided to make a break for it! Audaciously, they managed to hang on to the underside of a lorry delivering coal to the camp. When the vehicle slowed up at a road junction, they made a run for it, but this time they had decided to aim for the Swiss border, where in a desperate gamble to avoid the bitter cold, they trusted a local farmer to let them use his barn overnight. He sold them out to the Germans for a packet of cigarettes! They were marched back to the camp in the Black Forest, where they remained for the duration of the war. It proved not to be the best of experiences, as the food was dire, and heating consisted of one bucket of coal, per barracks, per week! On top of all this was the brutality of the guards, notably one guard in particular. This guard on one occasion, was given a work detail, which included my father-in-law Cyril, plus other six other inmates, to complete some farm work outside the prison camp. Cyril said this guard was a nasty bit of work and too free with his rifle butt! They managed to overpower the bullying guard, and after tying him up, they frog marched him back to the prison camp with his own rifle pointing at his back! The Commandant reminded them, he could have had them all executed for attacking the German guard, but in the event they had all got seven days solitary confinement instead. The guard disappeared shortly afterwards, with the rumour he was sent to the eastern front, where chances of survival were limited!

On a lighter side, there was humour too! The Germans were familiar with the British expression 'X' marks the spot'! The inmates would randomly make a cross in the quadrangle sand, and idly watch as the German guards frantically rushed around, digging where the various crosses were, in the vain hope of discovering a possible escape tunnel! Cyril said the scariest time was the last night of captivity. They heard the advancing American army by the roar of shells and bullets. The German guards were getting incredibly nervous, as they knew the game was up. Cyril said the allied prisoners were equally on edge, as they weren't sure whether the guards would open fire on them and run, or simply disappear into the night! Fortunately, they took the latter route! When the American soldiers arrived early the following morning, they had already killed some fleeing guards who refused to surrender.

Although Cyril had survived to tell the story, the damp,

cold living conditions badly affected his health, plus the poor-quality food, serviced by the guards, who frequently pinch some to supplement their own! He worked for a while after the war, but sadly passed away in 1981, at the age of sixty-one, a year before Joe was born. They were a courageous group of men and women fighting for the freedoms we sometimes take for granted. His endearing quirk was that he would NOT lend you a postage stamp. You had to buy it from him, but he would NEVER lend!

Towards the end of the eighties, we started to become restless and wanted to seek new adventures. This was aided and abetted by the decision of my wife's cousin, Anthony, his wife Jackie with their daughter and son-in-law, to move from their quaint but idyllic cottage, only two or three miles from our place in Kent, to Yorkshire, to start a Bed and Breakfast. They ended up, close to Robin Hood Bay, with a glorious old red tiled farmhouse with some twenty-five acres and outbuildings. Anthony had spent his working life at sea, as an officer in the merchant navy. Lately, he had worked on the cross channel ferries that plied between Dover and Calais, or the Zeebrugge route. Indeed, he was the first officer on the sister ship of the Herald of Free Enterprise, which tragically capsized and sank as it left the Zeebrugge port and entered the English Channel on the 6th March 1987, with the loss of one hundred and ninety three passengers and crew. It took just twenty seconds for the ferry to turn over onto its side. The outcome of the ensuing court case highlighted the huge risks with the roll on, roll off style of vessel, and plans were implemented to alter the lower deck levels to ensure future safety. Anthony and his family had left the ferry service just a few months before this tragedy, and were ensconced in their new home on the North York Moors. We desperately missed their company. They were a great couple with whom we spent a lot of happy times. Apart from the many house parties and frequent trips to London to see various theatre performances, Anthony, or Tone, as we affectionately called him, was Joe's Godfather, and my best friend. He had a great sense of humour, where if anything went wrong in his life, I would be to blame! He would always find a way to lump the blame on me. Mind you, I remember one occasion our respective wives had decided to have a 'girlie' night out. Subsequently, Tone turned up at our house 'Skeete' armed with a bottle of brandy and a porn video for us to watch! We settled down with the brandy and put the video on. Imagine our faces when a Donald Duck cartoon appeared! What was more depressing for Tone was that he parted company with twenty-nine pounds for this under the counter classic - apparently that was my fault too!

Their adventure to the north had made us restless too. Although grateful for the success of the transport business and the benefits it brought us, we both fancied a change of direction. After watching Tone, before their move to Yorkshire, make furniture in his spare time, I felt this could be a challenge, to utilise some artistic skill via cabinet-making and design. The transport business was sold quickly, and we managed to reshape our routine in the direction of making furniture. We already had the woodwork shop at home and a sales area within a supermarket precinct in Hythe, which was only a handful of miles from home. I had a two-pronged sales attack. Firstly, the sales area was to gain general public commissions, and secondly, I started targeting retail antique shops, as I designed Victorian-style book shelving and dressers. I made ten Victorian shelf units and gave them away as part of a promotional drive to attract the attention of retail shops. The strategy worked! Three agreed to either purchase from me or display in their shops, which immediately gave me more selling space, with no extra outlay!

This worked out well, especially not having to be at the Dover docks most nights in all weathers, loading the lorries! The trouble was, of course, our holidays had spoilt us in the glorious Cumbrian Lake District, and we still missed our dear relatives in Yorkshire. The matter came to a head on the day of Joe's first primary school sports day on Tayne Field, the local Lyminge playing field. We had agreed a selling price for our old farmhouse, and also a purchase price for a splendid farmhouse complete with the red pantile roof, at the head of a valley on the North York Moors, just six miles from our relatives. We could not believe the fantastic unbridled view across this valley, but unfortunately it was not to be! We suddenly found ourselves, on the day of exchanging contracts, caught up in the murky world of gazumping. The estate agent had organised a Dutch Auction, where we had merely been used as a tool, to raise the price to an existing prospective purchaser! We lost the property, but our biggest problem was, we had already promised the sale of our Kentish home! The following day, we had gone to Joe's primary school in Lyminge to watch him participate in his first ever sports day. It was a beautiful day, the sun shone as we sat watching Joe and his classmates haring up and down the obstacle course. The conversation drifted around to the dilemma of moving home, whether to look for another property in the north or just stay in Kent. It is strange how your life can turn in a split second based on one decision! To reinforce that moment in time, the St Etherburger Church bells peeled out the 3pm chimes, just as we made the final decision to move.

Hayley, having completed her book in 1988, alongside her friend Marcus, had a busy period with work in the second half of the eighties. To accompany the hugely popular "Parent Trap" she had made in 1961 for Disney, the "Parent

Trap 2" appeared in 1986, tailored as a television film, aimed initially at the American market. It premiered in July 1986 on the Disney Channel. It featured Hayley as the grown-up Susan and twin sister Sharon. It was a massive hit, resulting in "Parent Trap 3" in 1989, again with Hayley playing Susan Evers and Sharon Mckendrick, the twin sisters now married! This spawned the final instalment in 1989, entitled "Hawaiian Honeymoon", with Susan Evers now being Susan Wyatt! Between the two latter Parent Trap films, Hayley had a starring role alongside Peter Ustinov and Lauren Bacall in the film version of Agatha Christie's 1938 novel "Appointment with Death". It was produced and directed by Michael Winner, who also co-wrote the screenplay, alongside Peter Buckman and Anthony Shaffer. It was filmed on location in Israel during June, July and August 1988, with Hayley playing the eccentric archaeologist, 'Miss Quinton'. On completion of the film, she had to shoot over to the U.S.A. to do a show for 'The Arts Foundation' charity. Finally, Hayley returned to the UK to do an environmental pantomime for the 'Friends of the Earth' in London and Stratford. Soon, however, Hayley was again in front of the cameras, completing a television film in 1989 called "Back Home", based on the novel written by Michelle Magorian, with the screenplay completed by David Wood. It was a drama exploring the relationships within a family unit after being reunited at the end of the war in 1945.

While Hayley was incredibly busy in the late eighties, it had all changed for us in Kent. The old farmhouse had been sold, and we embarked on our new adventure in Cumbria, in 1988. We chose Cumbria, as we had built an affinity with the magnificent Lake District over the previous thirteen years. The countless times we had trekked up the side of Helvellyn, traversing the hazardous Striding Edge en route, to gaze in awe and wonderment at the grey mist that frequently and stubbornly stuck to the summit! I particularly remember gloomily standing by the side of Ullswater early one morning, staring at the grey still water of the lake and watching a pair of deer quietly grazing on the far side of the water. Within the hour, we would leave the peaceful haven of Glenridding and reluctantly point the car in the direction of the M6 and return to Kent. The nagging thought kept springing to mind, 'Not sure how, why or when, but somehow we will end up here'. The upshot was we didn't quite make the Lake District, or the North York Moors for that matter, having been gazumped. Indeed, even then, the Lake District property prices were astronomically high and totally out of our price range! However, by casting the net about, we had come across a glorious farmhouse near the town of Brampton in Cumbria. This property was advertised in a magazine. One of the problems at that time was that we were buying just at the wrong time. There had been a massive upsurge in property prices across the UK, fuelled by market needs. The upshot being the frequent, and frustrating, situation of finding the perfect property, only to have it immediately snatched away! To be fair, that also applied when we sold Skeete Place in Kent. It had gone on sale at 9am this particular day, and a guy banged on the door at 4pm who, incidentally, declined a guided tour, and then offered five thousand pounds more than the asking price, which meant Skeete Place was sold subject to contract! We eventually found 'Milestone House', on the Longtown Road between Brampton and Longtown, at a place called Newtown. It was a traditional Cumbrian farmhouse with a barn attached, which was converted into the dining room. It had a spacious five metre by five metre kitchen, complete with a walk-in larder. The living room was the width of the farmhouse, with the adjacent barn being the dining room. Joe's mum was over the moon with the kitchen, whilst my joy was the railway wagon workshop in the rear garden, where I could continue the cabinet-making business I had started in Kent. However, and it was massive 'however', we had not fully realised an inherent minus with the property. Not so much what it was, rather than where it was! We had only seen the property on two occasions, both on a Sunday. What we failed to appreciate was that the Longtown Road was then, in 1988, a busy route for traffic, in particular the heavy HGV's, who could shave a few miles off their journeys by following this road to the Scottish Borders instead of staying on the A69, through to the M6 and driving northbound. We found this out, having moved in, by being woken very early on that first Monday morning by the sound of heavy goods vehicles racing past our haven of peace at some sixty mph! As mentioned earlier, it was a traditional Cumbrian farmhouse, set in six acres to the rear, but with a tiny one and half metre front garden - the house shook every time a vehicle flew past, which was relentlessly frequent!

We lasted a year, mainly because we decided the situation, apart from the noise of wagons passing perilously close, was too dodgy, as Joe was only six at the time. And of course, we had great difficulty finding a buyer! Fortunately, the tenth couple who came to view wanted to start a market garden, and it suited their needs for passing traffic and land to cultivate. Result! In the meantime, my wife had spotted, through a Haltwhistle estate agent, a remote bungalow with several outbuildings, on the road between Hexham and Alston, high in the North Pennines, designated as an area of outstanding beauty. We totally fell in love with the property on our first visit, but not just the property, it was the stunning view commanded by its elevated position. At fifteen hundred feet, the vast North Pennine fells sprawled away from the property over unbelievable, breathtaking terrain. Even the old Roman fortress site, named Epiacum, was visible down in the valley. It suited all our needs and dreams. We envisaged a tearoom to exploit the view and aid the tourism business in the area, along with a craft centre to promote the Victorian furniture I was producing. The property, known as Clarghyll Head House, was ideally set approximately one hundred metres off the main road, with ample parking for visiting vehicles, plus a half-acre paddock for outside picnic tables and further parking if required. The small, tarmacked road stopped at the property, but continued as a public right of way known as the Drovers' Road. These were ancient roads that shepherds had used to move their flocks of sheep from fell to fell. This one, in particular, wound its way past the property, forever climbing, before disappearing into a pine forest and crossing into Northumbria. Needless to say, by the time we arrived back at Milestone House, we had made our minds up! We had seen it in August 1989, on a glorious sunny day, and it was idyllically perfect. By the end of September, we had moved to our dream location. Joe was enrolled at the local Alston Primary School. Although a relatively small town, with fewer than one thousand inhabitants, the locals dared anyone to call it a village! It was, by chartered consent, a market town, with trading rights established over many centuries by using the Market Cross in the centre of Alston. This town is unique in many ways. Its location is remote, possibly the most remote town in England, with Penrith to the west and Hexham to the north, both some twenty miles distant. Carlisle to the north-west is about thirty miles away. Alston lies at the meeting of two large valleys, which is the reason for its existence. Shepherds would bring their flocks to sell at the market and enjoy the ale in some of the twelve inns! Healthcare in the town was remarkable too. It has a medical centre, but sadly lost the small, attached cottage hospital with a dozen or so beds, set up with a five thousand pounds donation by Ruth Lancaster James, back in 1908.

Another big plus for Joe and myself, the town was also home to a narrow-gauge railway! Admittedly, it didn't go far back in 1989, but it was driven by steam locomotion, with all the attendant nostalgia, and also one diesel engine. Alston had been a branch line joining the mainline at Haltwhistle, but in the seventies the wisdom of the powers decreed it was not a sustainable line, and it was consequently axed. The South Tyneside Railway Preservation Society was set up with the intention of eventually getting the single track railway back to Haltwhistle, some twelve miles distant. This route is probably one of the most spectacular in Britain, bringing thousands of visitors to the area every year.

While we were busy converting the roadside barn at Clarghyll Head House into a tea shop, craft centre and workshop, through the horrendous winter of 1989, with the ever decreasing hope we would ever open for business by the following Easter, Hayley was gearing up for her part as 'Anna' in "The King and I". This was another collaboration between the famous musical duo Rodgers and Hammerstein, inspired by Margaret Landon's novel, 'Anna and the King of Siam', written in 1944, and based on the memoirs of a British governess Anna Leonowens in thc 1860's, and her on/off relationship with the King of Siam. The musical was planned to tour Australia starting June 1991 in South Australia, followed by Western Australia, Queensland, New South Wales and Victoria, and finishing in February 1992. She had written before going to Australia to say she was departing on the 24th April. Although it was a lengthy run, she expected to get a two month break in the summer to return home. Where possible, and of course alongside her family and friends, I would try to make sure Hayley had a bouquet of flowers on the opening night. The first night is always a stressful event at any level of entertainment. First of all, you hope you have an audience, which is always a good start! You desperately hope the audience likes the production, and equally, it is hoped the theatre critics are having a good night, and rate your performance positively! The show was a smash hit and enjoyed adoration at every venue!

After working through the terrible weather conditions through the 1989 winter at our lofty home in the North Pennines, where we experienced total white-outs with increased frequency and intensity, we finally managed to be ready for our grand opening in the spring of 1990. Like any other business, the world was not waiting for us to open our tea shop! Publicity is essential, and we obtained this by contacting and networking with the local information point, and becoming associated with other like-minded crafts folk and, basically, joining in. As part of this strategy, we attended one of the Alston Moor Schools Association meetings, an organisation with the primary objective to raise funds for the one secondary and two primary schools on the Moor.

While at this well attended event held in the local Samuel Kings Secondary School, the chairman Rex Horrocks, a very liked and respected member of the teaching staff, posed the question directed at us, the newcomers (or more quaintly the 'incomers'. We were not alone, there were a few other 'incomer' families present!)

"How about the new people at the back of the hall? Have any of you got any new fundraising ideas to bring to the table?" Heads swung in our general direction. Before I could prevent it happening, my wife shoved my hand in the air and exclaimed in my ear how impressed I had been with the duck race at Joe's previous Irthington Primary School.

"Yes, well er, a duck race?" I said. This suggestion was met with a ripple of amusement!

"Oh gosh! Have you already run a duck race?" The thought suddenly flashed through my mind, the River Tyne flowed past the foot of the town, so obviously, yes, they would already be running such a race!

"No, we have never tried that idea! We have the water for sure, so yes, I think you might be on to something there!"

This was the birth of the Alston duck race, which was to run annually until 2015, raising thousands of pounds for local schools. It was usually held on the evening of the last day of the school year, so it attracted a large but exuberant audience, who were in the mood to back the thousands of plastic ducks thrown from the local river bridge and floated to the finishing line some quarter of a mile further down the river. The local firefighters would put a net across the river to catch the ducks.

Latterly, I had a shop in the town, and it was a good outlet for selling the duck race tickets. However, I had to keep a straight face when selling tickets to a tourist who initially asked whether we used live ducks! In my mind's eye, I envisaged a thousand ducks lined ready for the off - imagine yelling at duck 872, to get him back in line! Not sure how I suppressed my mirth when she asked whether we used a starting pistol! Again, in my mind's eye, I could see a thousand ducks taking off in all directions to their new-found freedom! Another time, a gent came into the shop and looked at some books we had for sale. I approached him to inquire whether he would like to buy a fifty-pence ticket to support local children. His answer was swift and succinct:

"I have come into your shop to browse, NOT to be solicited for gambling!"

"Gosh! I do apologise."

"I will now leave your shop, and never return!"

I became involved with AMSA, helping with the Spring and Christmas Fairs, and musical forays. It helped dispel the notion that the dangerous Confederates from the south, who lived on top of the hill, were indeed a threat to local culture!

The Clarghyll Head Craft and Teashop gradually gained momentum. My wife looked after the teashop, and I made the furniture. By then, we had four dogs, and it was such a blessing to walk two or three times a day up the track into Northumbria. The view looking towards the Cheviots was amazing. The last winter had been particularly harsh, with up to seven feet of snow, which at times, totally covered the door. It was strange, opening that door to confront a solid white wall! I had to cut steps into said white wall to get out. I did this by passing buckets of snow back to Joe and his mum, who walked through the home to the bathroom and dumped it in the bath to thaw, and drain away. The other blessing we were on fell water rather than mains water, meaning a natural, but constant underground supply. We never experienced the problem of freezing pipes, as in this country water does not normally freeze if it is more than ten inches underground! But I still had to brave the elements to retrieve the logs from the nearby barn, to keep the home fires burning.

It was a rude awakening when we first moved to Clarghyll, during the previous autumn. The first job in the barn, destined to be the teashop, was removing a serious amount of duck and chicken poo! Imagine a barn fifty-five by twenty-five feet wide, with poo approximately six feet deep on one end, dropping to one foot the other end. A ginormous wedge of poo, and all to shovel by hand! We were lucky, as we found a chap in Slaggyford, a small village about nine or ten miles distant, who was happy to collect it with his tractor and trailer. It occupied us for about two weeks! Mind, it was beautiful manure; it had been there for many years and was well rotted down. The added bonus, hidden by the mountain of poo, was the exposed cobbled interior floor to the barn and the original loose box doors. Tone had come over from North Yorkshire to lend his expertise in developing the interior beamed ceiling and the mock Tudor style timber supports. The autumn was fairly mild, with spectacular sunsets over the far fells. Of course, this was the lull before the Pennine winter set in. The hardest part for me during that snowy winter was reconstructing a building attached to the teashop, destined to be the toilet area. It had no roof and was bereft of a few courses of stone walling. My wife kept me sane by keeping up a steady supply of hot coffee, to prevent the icy grip of the bitter northerly winds from destroying my will to live! There were times when I had to squat behind the wall I was repairing, purely to escape the insane blast from the north. Eventually, by March 1990, the roof was restored, and it seemed like heaven, being sheltered under cover to complete the final fixings. As previously mentioned, we opened at Easter that year. During that period, we learned a lot about retailing and marketing, which made us better prepared for the 1991 season. We had spent the winter months making more furniture stock and sourcing new wholesalers for craft jewellery, copperware, pottery and fabrics. We spent our free time with Joe, exploring the fells near our home, and sometimes driving back to the Brampton area where we previously lived, to revisit Talkin Tarn, a beautiful natural lake left over from the glacier days. Many happy hours were spent strolling around the one and a half mile tarn walk, complete with its small island connected by a wooden bridge. On one memorable walk after we dropped Joe off at his primary school, we took our three dogs, and followed the scenic route around the tarn. On the eastern side, there is a steep bank, ideal for lobbing sticks up, giving the dogs the opportunity to race and retrieve them. Sadly, on this occasion, Sam, our beautiful, long coated German Shepherd, got it wrong. Having got to the stick first, he careered down the bank at a zillion miles per hour and crashed into me. Bearing in mind he weighed just a tad under eight stone, I immediately collapsed on top of him. But what I hadn't noticed, in my vain attempt to keep balanced, was that my arms had swung out, and I accidentally punched Joe's mum in the face!!! When I got to my feet, the dog was out of breath, I was rubbing my knee, and Joe's mum was nursing her jaw! Just a handful of miles away was another one of our favourite walks, known as the Geltsdale woods. A tree covered, deep valley, carved by the River Gelt, with a series of magnificent waterfalls, following the river course. The amazing spectacle in the autumn was watching the salmon return to their spawning ground by leaping up the waterfalls.

By the arrival of spring 1991, Hayley had left for Australia, and after spending several weeks rehearsing, finally enjoyed a fantastic first night with rave reviews. She wrote a letter thanking us all for the first night's flowers, and hoped we were all well in our Cumbrian retreat, and having a successful second season. Up at our lofty perch at Clarghyll, we were doing well. People from the previous year returned once again, to sit outside on the patio and drink their tea or coffee. They studied the magnificent vista of the fells, with their ever-changing colours, as the clouds created hues of untold beauty. We also had some locals from Alston who became regulars. One chap used to come up every Sunday morning to read his paper outside with a coffee. As we were on the old Drovers' Road, we had a few hikers come our way who would occasionally pitch their tent for the night. Some stayed longer. It was an idyllic position, a dream of freedom and space. Joe's mum enjoyed the freedom too. She was independent, she could drive. I had a van for my timber materials, and she had a car. Somewhere in early June 1991, Joe's mum decided to visit her mother in Kent. Joe was still at school with the prospect of the long summer holiday coming over the hill in July, and it made sense for her to visit

Kent before the school holiday got under way. With local help, it was possible to juggle the teashop, workshop and conjure up various ways of cooking beans on toast. Thank goodness for school meals! We both wished her a safe journey, with hugs and kisses, as we waved her off on the road to the south. We also asked her to let us know she had arrived safely, but please, please bring back some Folkestone rock to get our teeth into!

The snow of the winter was quickly consigned to the history books, as the June sun shone on our lofty haven. The taxi would collect Joe and a couple of other children living in various other isolated homes about half eight in the morning. I would busy myself making sure the tearoom and the outside patio were clean and tidy, plus the toilet block, which looked so innocent in the summer sun, opposed to the nightmare snow-bound building site it had been, just eighteen months before! Talking about toilets, it creased me up with laughter on one occasion, after a chap had parked his car and went straight to the toilet block, which was innocent enough, but re-emerged a few seconds later carrying one of our twenty-four packs of toilet rolls! He actually tipped-toed past the shop window. It was pure comedy, and to be honest, I couldn't be bothered to chase after him as I was laughing so much!

We employed the services of a friend we had made in Alston, who would help on odd occasions. She would arrive about ten, just in time for the morning coffee customers. This would run into the lunches, followed by the afternoon teas, with exceedingly fine cakes made by my wife! Time was always allocated when Joe returned from school to do kids' and dad's stuff. We were fortunate to have a ditch running down the hill to the main road, which was always flowing well with water. Super for model boat races, or for getting into scientific mode; we actually built a hydro-electric power system, using an old bicycle wheel, a bit of guttering and other bits and pieces, which generated enough power to run a torch bulb! We gazed in awe at this invention as dusk approached.

The days soon passed, with Joe and I looking forward to the regular evening chats with his mum. She enjoyed her time in Folkestone, visiting friends and relatives. Towards the end of her week, she mentioned that her great friend from her school days was returning with her for a short break with her son. Joe was so excited when the day finally came for his mum to return, as indeed was I. We had arranged she would ring from Barnard Castle, before the last leg of the drive across the Pennines back to Alston. Joe asked whether we could surprise them by driving a few miles to a place called the Ashgill Falls, a spectacular waterfall underneath the road bridge, where his mum would shortly be passing on her way home. While we waited, the pair of us hung over the bridge parapet to admire the view. The waterfall had a drop of some eighty feet on the south side of the bridge. It was possible to follow a rocky footpath down to the waterfall, where you could actually walk behind this magnificent sheet of water, and even take photographs through the waterfall.

"Look Dad, I can see mum's car, she's coming," cried an exuberant Joe. Sure enough, I could make the white Mazda, making the long descent from the fells to the bridge. She pulled up with lots of smiles, and her two passengers were waving too. Desperate for a cuppa and a loo, she wanted to get home. Somehow it felt just right to have her back again. Over the following few days, the three of them did a bit of sight-seeing, while Joe was at school and I was back in the teashop. We would play games later, after Joe returned from school. The same pattern was followed on the evening of Tuesday 2nd July 1991. After tea, games and a bit of telly,

Joe went to bed, as did the other two guests. My wife and I were left in the kitchen, and as we both enjoyed a game of cards, I produced the pack, and we started to play. After a few hands of rummy, it became apparent she was feeling a little downcast.

"You okay?" I enquired, "you seem a bit quiet".

"I thought I would take my friends back tomorrow."

"Gosh, that's another long journey there and back. Will you stop over for a couple of days again, with your mum?"

"In a manner of speaking," there was a short pause before she uttered the most devastating words of my life, "But I am not coming back."

It was as simple as that! Six words and our lives changed forever. Obviously, we talked for hours. She explained how somehow she felt she had lost her identity. She was someone's wife, someone's mum, but not her own person. In my innocence, when she said she had no intention of returning, I immediately took it as read she was taking Joe with her. Apparently, that option was not part of her plan. To this day, I believe she was having some sort of emotional breakdown. One of her endearing qualities was her honesty, meaning what you saw was what you got! But this one I genuinely did not understand. We sat talking until the early hours, but she was resolute with her intention, and would leave in the morning. After she had gone to bed, I wandered out into our garden. Being early July, it was getting light even at 2am. I stood and watched six deer munching grass in the adjacent field, desperately trying to make sense of this terrible situation. No big drama, no screaming abuse or even raised voices. Proof positive was that no-one came dashing out into the kitchen to see what the noise was about! In a calm and collected fashion, she declared she did not like the area, the people, the weather, the tearoom, or any of it. My suggestion to return to Kent was not an option, as I too was an obstacle to her future happiness!

"You can fall in love with a person, but equally, you can fall out of love too." She had said.

"And Joe?" was the burning question.

"Of course, I love Joe to bits, but it will be problematic to get a job and take care of myself, and besides, his school and friends are up here"

In a total daze, I finally tumbled into bed alongside my wife, exhausted, but unable to sleep with so much on my mind. Thirteen years of happy marriage. Our joy when Joe was born after being told having a child was possibly not going to happen. The excitement when we moved north. I lay there, analysing past conversations we'd had, trying to make sense of any of it. Clearly, I had missed the signs! Eventually, I dozed, but was disturbed by the noise of the bedroom door opening. Joe's timing could not have been worse! He had got up early to make his mum and dad breakfast in bed. He sported a tray of cereals and two tumblers of orange juice. When he had left the bedroom, I turned to his mum, giving her a gentle nudge to wake her up.

"Am I having a bad dream or something? Our conversation last night?"

She sat up, in the bed, staring out of the bedroom window, across to where the deer had been grazing, and confirmed her decision to leave after breakfast, having a shower and packing a few things. She would tell Joe just before departing.

While she was having a shower, and seeing Joe playing in the garden with the friend's son, I thought I would make her friend aware of what was happening, and also make arrangements to leave. Everything was becoming abundantly clear when the friend declared:

"You have to get it into your head, your marriage is over and she is not coming back!"

She already knew! The whole point of the friend accompanying my wife was to support her decision to leave. They left at ten that morning. I will not dwell on the hugely emotional and traumatic scene inflicted on our son when she explained she was leaving. Other than that, Joe and I both shared the terrible joint grief of losing someone we dearly loved. We watched as she disappeared down the main road towards Alston and to the subsequent long journey back to Kent. Then we retreated into our front room, and I sat cuddling our nine year-old lad until four-thirty that afternoon! I must admit my brain had a problem computing what had happened over the last twelve hours before she had left. At the start of the evening, we were playing cards. A married couple with their nine year-old lad tucked up in bed, after a pleasant day with the two friends, who had also retired to bed. We had this incredibly, stunning home, set in the magnificent North Pennines, designated an ‘area of outstanding beauty’, with our business just starting to flourish during its second season. Dramatically, overnight I went from a happily married family man to a single parent, who, from the word go, had to actively support his son. Joe's life was turned upside down by his mother's sudden decision to leave. The whole drama hit me like a hammer blow once Joe had gone to bed that night. Even going to bed itself was quite traumatic for Joe. I stayed with him that first night, sleeping in an armchair in his bedroom, as he was convinced he would get up in the morning, and I would have gone too. I assured him no, I emphatically promised him that would never happen, whatever the future had in store. Later that evening, after Joe had fallen asleep, I had to get up to visit the bathroom. Afterwards, I made a quick cup of tea. When I sat alone in the front room, the floodgates just opened! I felt suddenly so alone, being hundreds of miles from my family. The nearest family was my wife's cousin Tone and his wife Jackie, near Robin Hood Bay, in North Yorkshire. Having regained composure, I phoned and explained the situation to Tone. His immediate response was that he would drive over the next day, adding with his dry sense of humour:

"I'm not bothered about you - you're big and ugly enough to take care of yourself! Joe is my godson, so I worry about him! See you tomorrow about lunchtime."

The following morning, I had phoned the school to inform them of the situation and why he had not attended school the previous day. The school was fantastic and said keep him off for as long as you need, especially as the long summer holiday was looming in two or three weeks. Understandably, Joe was very subdued that first morning. It was breaking my heart to watch Joe walk around the kitchen, clutching A.G.Bear, his favourite teddy he had been given for his second birthday. A.G. still lives with me to this day. Mind you, he now wears spectacles, and has trouble zipping up his jacket!

Tone, as promised, duly turned up at lunchtime, armed with a bottle of brandy, which he set on the kitchen table with fine panache.

"When Joe has gone to bed this evening, you and me 'Wrighty' will have a drink or three!"

Among other terms of endearments, such as 'You old Bastard', he frequently referred to me as 'Old Wrighty!'

"But for now, the three of us are going to Talkin Tarn for lunch. Oh, by the way Wrighty, you're paying!"

Having Tone descend on us was the exact medicine Joe and I needed to restore some sort of normality in our shattered lives. He stayed with us for three days before returning to Yorkshire. The family on both sides were supportive, and equally shocked at the news, as they had seen us as a rock-solid couple reading from the same sheet. I clung to the forlorn belief that given the space, she might return, even if it meant Joe and me returning to Kent too. Sadly, it became abundantly clear that even if we returned to Kent, there was no possibility of reconciliation. To be fair to Joe's mum, she has been a brilliant grandmother to our two grandchildren over the years, taking them on holidays and helping whenever she could. By chance, Joe's work took him back to Kent, and not a million miles from where his mum lives. He also has her wicked sense of black humour. On a visit up here last year, which was the thirtieth anniversary of the breakup, Joe suddenly came out with this observation:

"Dad, hasn't the penny dropped yet?"

"I'm sorry?"

"Well, first mum moved off back to Kent, then I did. And here you are, some four hundred miles away. Result!"

Naturally, we had to put the Clarghyll Head property on the market, as Joe's mum needed funds to buy her own place, as she was currently staying with her mother.

It was a summer where Joe and I had to make many adjustments to our new life - he was my priority. We took time out to have fun days together. If I could not get help for the shop, I would simply shut it! In the event, local people were amazing and helped wherever possible. Joe's mum had walked out on the 3rd July 1991, with the property sold, subject to contract, on the August Bank Holiday, 26th August 1991.

The couple who bought Clarghyll Head House, Peter and Anne Lascelles, were an extraordinary family. Peter's sister is Jane Fearnley-Whittingstall, famed for her gardening designs and her "Good Granny Guide" plus "The Good Granny Cookbook". She is also the mother of T.V presenter, Hugh Fearnley-Whittingstall. Peter himself was educated at St. Paul's school in London, gaining entry into Eton, and ultimately Oxford University, where he gained both a history and biology degree. He then returned to St. Paul's as a teacher, where he remained until early retirement. The move to Cumbria allowed Peter to follow another passion for making pottery in the shop we had created. He became quite renowned for his unique pottery designs, leading to a constant flow of orders. Peter's wife Anne had an equally intriguing history. She and her three siblings were the children of Christopher Serpell, the BBC journalist covering the Cuban crisis in the early sixties. He interviewed John Kennedy and Fidel Castro during his time in the USA. I can remember listening to his daily news bulletins on the radio in the early sixties, as the world appeared to be lurching towards another catastrophic world war. Fortunately for mankind, it was averted! Interestingly, during World War Two, Chris was on war operations where his immediate boss was Ian Flemming of James Bond fame, and it was him who suggested Chris become a television journalist! Both Peter and Anne, and their family, became close friends until sadly, Peter passed away in 2014, followed by Anne in 2019. It was an honour to be asked to write and present her eulogy in the beautiful Hexham Abbey. Over the years, I had come to know her well enough to dish the dirt on some comedic events celebrating her life, but her sister, Francesca, contributed a fitting poem written by Anne herself, entitled "Love", which summed up her love for her husband and children well. The eulogy finished by quoting a line from a Philip Larkin poem: "whatever will remain of me is love".

Leaving Clarghyll would prove to be another pivotal point in mine, and Joe's life.

8 THE TIMES ARE A CHANGIN'

While Joe and I were coming to terms with our new life in Cumbria, Hayley was having runaway success with the "The King and I" production, completing their comprehensive Australian Tour. It had received rave reviews at every venue where it had performed. Even though Hayley was on the opposite side of the planet, there was no exception to my tradition of sending her, where possible, a bouquet of flowers on the opening night. Prophetically, Hayley sat down and wrote to us on the 2nd July, not only thanking us for the bouquet, but also writing a newsy letter regarding the progress of the production. While she wrote this in Australia, Joe's mum was busy telling me that our marriage was at an end! Close to the end of July, I wrote to Hayley explaining the home situation. A few days later, having had a brilliant day out with Joe in Carlisle, exploring the castle and the Tully House Museum, we were back at home relaxing and playing games, when the telephone rang.

"Hello, is that Trevor Wright?" a woman's voice enquired.

"It certainly is."

"This is Mary, Hayley's mum. Hayley regularly rings us and mentioned your recent marital problems. I hope you don't mind, John and I were talking about you and Joe, so I thought I would call to make sure you are both alright."

What a wonderful gesture, and it has never been forgotten. It speaks volumes about the loving and caring nature the Mills family possesses. The conversation lasted for twenty minutes or so. We didn't get immersed in the negativity of the break-up, but spoke more about Joe and his various activities, and how the local Alston townsfolk had been incredibly supportive. It really lifted my spirits to talk with her. I briefly saw her as the bride's mum at Cowden Village Church, back in 1961, when Juliet got married, but we had never actually met. I feel so blessed that Ivy Fountain had sent me on the farm mission to Cowden all those years ago!

Sir John and Lady Mills lived at Hills House, in Denham, having bought it in 1975. At some point in the forties, Merle Oberon and her producer husband, Alexander Korda, had occupied the imposing 17th Century Netherlandish Classicism residence. In the early years of being a struggling actor, Hayley's dad would daydream of owning the house as he walked past the property on the way to work at the nearby Beaconsfield Film Studios. In the event, they stayed in Hills House until 2004, when with failing health, particularly for Mary, it was considered expedient to move to a bungalow in Denham. Before owning Hills House, the Mills family owned Sussex House Farm in Cowden and also a flat in London. They decided to sell both properties towards the latter part of 1963, to realise their dream of returning to their beloved home on Richmond Hill, called "The Wick", where they had also lived several years previously. Built in 1775, The Wick, a beautiful Grade 1 example of Georgian architecture, is set in a magnificent position on Richmond

Hill, with views across to the Thames. They eventually sold it to Ronnie Wood of The Rolling Stones, where later it was sold to Pete Townshend of The Who fame. How odd to think that on a few occasions, I was part of the warm-up act for The Who, during my rock era in the sixties.

My personal favourite film, starring Hayley in her younger days, was unquestionably "Whistle Down The Wind", beautifully written by her mum, Mary Hayley Bell, in 1959. Originally, she wrote the story based around the Reigate, Dorking area in Surrey. When the idea was conceived for it to be made into a film, the screenwriters Keith Waterhouse and Willis Hall decided to relocate the story to the north, in Lancashire. The high Pennine Fells, with their damp and sombre greyness, lent themselves immaculately to the plot, especially as it was also filmed in black and white, which added to the atmosphere. Bryan Forbes had done a brilliant job of directing the film, drawing on the parallels between the Bible and the storyline.

Basically, a group of young innocent children had found a man they thought to be Jesus in a barn on their farm. He was actually a desperate man on the run from the police, suspected of killing someone. The youngsters gave him food, but the secret could not be contained anymore, especially with more children hearing, and captivated by the 'miracle'. Of course, the truth eventually came out. One of the final, poignant scenes was a long shot of "Jesus" silhouetted against the skyline with his arms stretched out, surrounded by the arresting police. Clearly drawing a parallel to Jesus's disciples, the constant spiritual battle between right and wrong, and betrayal resulting in the crucifixion. The film premiered on 20th July 1961. It was nominated for four BAFTA awards, including Hayley's for Best British Actress, Bryan Forbes for Best Director, Keith Waterhouse and Willis Hall for Best British screenwriters, and Bryan Forbes again for Best Film from any source. The budget was set at approximately £150,000 and turned in a profit of just shy of £240,000 by 1971. This was the follow up film to Hayley's massive success with Disney's "Pollyanna", which premiered in 1960.

Hayley had arrived home from her successful Australian tour of "The King and I", at the back end of 1991. However, it was not long before she was offered the part of Jane Banbury in Noel Coward's "Fallen Angels", which toured in 1992. A big plus, as Hayley performed with her sister Juliet, and even a bigger plus, it was coming to a theatre relatively near us, The Forum Theatre at Billingham. It was a bright and sunny autumn day late in October when Joe and I drove over the fells from Alston, winding our way through the Wear Valley, passing on our way, the famous Killhope Lead Mining Museum in County Durham, complete with its 10.3 metre diameter working water wheel, which was fed from a man-made reservoir situated on higher ground, to enable this amazing grinding machine to operate. Joe and I had been there two or three times with his primary school. Great fun and enlightening to enter the old mine and experience what the working conditions were like in the middle of the nineteenth century! The mine is well lit for the tourism trade, but when the group reaches a certain point, the lights are extinguished, and the guide lights a tallow candle attached to his hat, to demonstrate the utter blackness of the working conditions! Utterly terrifying, and not for anyone who suffers from claustrophobia!

Our journey continued through the valley towns of Stanhope, with its ancient, petrified stone tree and amazing stepping stones across the River Wear. We progressed through Wolsingham, and by crossing over the A68 roundabout to Crook, passed Tony Blair's future constituency of Sedgefield, before reaching Billingham, which lies just north east of Stockton close to the River Wear. By the time we had parked at the Forum Theatre, both Joe and I were certainly looking forward to the show and meeting with Hayley backstage afterwards, which I had prearranged with her. The play was written in 1925 by Noel Coward, who was actually one of Juliet's Godparents, alongside Sir Laurence Olivier and his wife, Viven Leigh. Both Juliet and Hayley turned in impeccable and delightful performances. Although an incredibly witty play, it was an acute observation of the way women were treated in the post war years of the mid-twenties. Women had, of course, played an invaluable part in the war effort, especially as so many menfolk had volunteered or been conscripted into the army, and sadly became casualties of the horrendous 1914-1918 conflict. When peacetime finally arrived, the menfolk expected, or rather demanded, the ladies return to their duties in the kitchen and bedroom, with very little say in how they could conduct their lives. Society, both locally and globally, was shocked that women enjoyed drinking and wearing more practical clothes, as opposed to traditional crinolines. There is a wonderful scene in the play where Hayley and Juliet, playing Jane Banbury and Julia Sterrol respectively, get totally drunk at the dinner table. It starts as a normal, refined meal, which descends into a drunken debacle, where the two women flick peas across the table at each other! Watching that scene alone reinforced the fact that you witnessed acting royalty performing on the stage. Joe certainly enjoyed the pea-throwing antics!

After the show, we located the stage door, armed with my note from Hayley inviting me backstage. She must have forewarned the door attendant, as he knew we would be arriving. He made a quick call to her dressing room. She would be out as soon as she had changed into 'civvies'. Less than ten minutes later, Hayley appeared at the rear door with a beaming face. After the traditional peck on the cheek and giving Joe a hug, she asked:

"Have you two eaten? I am absolutely famished. Shall we pop out for a quick bite, there's a pub close to here in the precinct?"

This was not expected, and it rounded the day off very pleasantly, sitting in the pub, just the three of us, having pub grub and a regular natter. Hayley was adept at engaging Joe in conversation, having had plenty of experience with her own sons, Crispian and Jason. Apart from Hayley asking Joe directly whether he had enjoyed the show, to which he referred straight away to the pea-throwing scenario, we, again, tended to talk about everything else going on with the planet. Interestingly, whilst having this chat over our snack, I noticed a group of people gradually gathering at a polite distance from our table. Eventually, when we got up to leave, we were suddenly engulfed by this enthusiastic group of people. I immediately stood back with Joe, slightly behind Hayley, acknowledging this was part of her professional life. Several people were pushing serviettes, pieces of paper, and even a newspaper, for Hayley to sign. None of this fazed her whatsoever! She was absolutely charming to them all and answered a range of questions. It was such an interesting insight into the life of a famous person. It is a strange phenomenon. I was obviously aware of Hayley's prominence on the world stage, but to me, she was, and still is, a lady with a wonderful warm and approachable personality.

"Why did that man shake your hand dad?" asked the ever observant and inquisitive Joe.

"I have absolutely no idea Joe," I replied. He was, in fact, one of the chaps in the little group of people, who suddenly turned in my direction, grabbed my hand and shook it vigorously! He might have reasoned that, as Hayley was famous, it seemed obvious, anyone she accompanied would also be famous, even though he couldn't actually place me in any play or film! On the other hand, it could simply have been the old concept, 'you lucky old devil'!

We walked back to the stage door of the Forum Theatre, said our goodbyes, and having watched Hayley disappear into the shadows of the theatre's interior, and world of make-believe, Joe and I ambled back to the car, which was patiently waiting for us to retrace our steps back to the high fells of Alston. It had been a great day out and a glimpse of celebrity culture. A fitting sequel to this anecdote was, whilst waiting for Hayley, her sister walked past to the exit! She smiled, and I just grinned!

Just a few years before our visit to the Forum theatre, I planned a treat to take Joe on a visit to the "Emmerdale" Studios near Leeds, as we were both big fans of the show. Joe's mum was still about at this point, but although she enjoyed and followed the story lines, she just fancied having some time out with the dogs, on the fells close to home. The interior studio sets for the production were housed in a wonderful redundant Victorian woollen mill named Farsley Mill, not far from Pudsey, near Leeds, with the village exterior location being filmed in the Dales, at Esholt. Due to vast crowds visiting Esholt to catch a glimpse of the actors of this famous 'soap', it was difficult to keep to the demanding film schedule. Therefore, it was decided to move the exterior location to a purpose built village on the Harewood Estate, close to Wetherby, in 1997. Farsey Mill remained the interior studio until 2001, when they were relocated to the Yorkshire Television Studios, situated in the Kirkstall Road part of Leeds.

It was a great day out for the pair of us. We had become members of the Emmerdale official fan club, which is why we had been advised a visit was being organised. Incidentally, Joe and I held the record of being "Emmerdale's" highest viewers in England! Our home in Alston stood at exactly fifteen hundred feet above sea level! Fame indeed! The tour started with a warm welcome from a member of the production staff. After getting the introductions out of the way, our group of about twenty were initially ushered into an exceedingly dishevelled office, where we were told this was the habitat of the scriptwriters, who would huddle together, drink copious amounts of coffee, whilst agonising over the ongoing story lines. There were various pens, pencils and writing pads, strewn over the long table, which dominated the room. It certainly looked like a work in progress, sort of scenario! The thought occurred to me that perhaps the half full cigarette ashtrays were merely props to promote the realism!

The next port of call was the Green Room, where the cast members either seek quiet sanctuary to rehearse their lines between scenes, or are asked by the director to sit there while set changes are made. From here, we were ushered into a series of three-sided sets instantly recognisable, ranging from Annie Sugden's famous farmhouse kitchen to the Woolpack Public Bar, complete with real beer pumps. Apparently, the only way to get a decent replica of the beer was to have the real thing! Mind, a few unmentioned characters got a little worse for wear when several 'takes' were necessary! We were all encouraged to explore the various sets and take photographs. It was fairly obligatory to take a picture of Joe pulling a pint! It was explained to us all that the sets were three-sided where the action would be, leaving the cameras to take their shots. The guide said the main continuity errors were the wall clocks and the outside views seen through the windows. The former had regular discrepancies, as the clock kept ticking despite any cut in filming, and the latter focused on the seasonal variations of spring, summer, autumn and winter, which sometimes was inadvertently overlooked by the continuity technicians, with the hilarious view of both winter and summer visible from the same room! Another error would be an exterior scene depicting severe weather conditions, where the actor would be totally drenched, then switching to an interior scene where, magically, he is bone dry!

The other encounter I personally had with the "Emmerdale " production team, was at the Queens Hotel in Leeds in 1990, where a fundraising event was being held for the benefit of the local children's hospital. Being a member of the "Emmerdale " club, twenty dining seats had been allocated to members and my name got drawn from the hat! Obviously, I could take my wife, but she declined as it would be late to drive back home and she preferred to spend time with Joe. It was a great evening. On the Farsley Mill tour there were no members of the cast present, but at the Queen's they were there en bloc! My table was shared with "Kim Tate" the lady up at "Home Farm", or rather Clare King the actress, and I was back-to-back with Chris Chittell, alias "Mr. Pollard", who had started his career back in 1967 in the iconic film "To Sir With Love", playing the teenage lad 'Potter', in a tough London school. Lulu portrayed a female classmate, and Sidney Poiitier played the teacher. The chap to my immediate right during the meal, who had worked for years on the production sets. He was exceedingly articulate and entertaining, regaling me for most of the evening with seriously funny anecdotes concerning the "Emmerdale Production".

Having sold the family home on top of the Clarghyll Fells following my wife's departure, Joe and I had moved into an extraordinary house in the Butts in Alston town centre. It consisted of three buildings, being linked together over the centuries. The three-storey stone house, facing the Butts, was built in 1732 and became known as The Greyhound pub and guest house. To the rear of the property, there was originally a detached cottage built in 1611, which had outside steps leading to the living quarters for the shepherd, with his sheep housed downstairs, beneath him. An early type of central heating! These two buildings were linked together in Victorian times, resulting in an unusual architectural mixture. Internally, it was equally fascinating, especially the kitchen floor, which had a gradient of four inches from one side to the other, which made things a trifle difficult when serving soup! The whole building was heavily beamed, which really complemented the idea for a craft shop and tearoom. The latter had an exterior door out into a quiet courtyard, where customers could sup their coffee or tea. Interestingly, it was an upside-down house, insomuch as the shop was on the ground floor, with the bedrooms above and the living room up another flight of stairs. Nothing was straight! Wonky walls, illogical passages, nooks and crannies, but Joe and I both loved it. We spent many happy years running the shop, which incorporated thirty-two local craft workers to supply us with their wares.

Fame came to the building in 1999, when one Sunday morning, a gentleman approached me at the counter and exclaimed:

"This would make a fantastic workhouse!"

"Oh gosh, it looks that rough, does it? But actually, it's my home!"

The young man smiled and continued;

"Hi, I am Martin Jay. I work for Diplomatic Films as a locations manager. We are planning to film Alan Bleasdale's adaptation of "Oliver Twist" here in Alston, and this would seriously transform into an excellent home and workhouse for Mr and Mrs Bumble. Interested? We pay, of course, and it goes without saying, reinstate the building after completion of the film, as we would have to dress the building down."

I would lose the shop for about two weeks, but would be accordingly reimbursed. The bedrooms directly above the shop would be needed and turned into a drawing room. There would be some disruption with cameramen, lighting and sound guys constantly on the move, but it sounded exciting, so I agreed! The set construction team moved in about a week before the cast and technical crew. The middle of Alston was quickly transformed. All telephone poles and lines vanished, as did traffic parking lines. The Co-op, the centrepiece of the town, became the custom shed, which is ironic, as Alston is one thousand feet above sea level! Two metal swing gates were forged and fitted across the entrance to the Butts, to give the appearance of a workhouse yard. Close by, was the centuries old market cross, a monument, which required very little set dressing. It has historically dominated the centre of Alston, where in 1748, John Wesley stood on the steps preaching his religious philosophy. Even to this day, it still has its charter to trade, where locals are permitted to sell their wares under cover. Straw was scattered to disguise the rain drains. Someone commented Alston had been dragged kicking and screaming into the 1830s! Even the semi derelict building next to my shop had a huge porch added to become the workhouse entrance.

Finally, the big day arrived when the Circus hit the town! Some cast were put into holiday caravans by the railway, some at local hotels. The town hall was totally taken over by the one hundred and twenty local sourced support artists who mustered first thing each morning to initially get into costume and then proceed through makeup with a scheduled 10am start at the location. No mean feat by any standard!

Meanwhile, I was back at home acting like a security guard. There were so many technicians going upstairs and downstairs, with a focal point being my bedroom, which was quickly cleared to transform into a drawing room for Mr and

Mrs Bumble, in their home above the workhouse. The director, Renny Rye, was getting extremely concerned about the number of people just entering the building and hovering. He thought they were local people who I knew, and conversely I believed they were people connected to the film set! I spent an hour or so diplomatically asking various people to leave and watch the location shoot from behind the cameras, on the opposite side of the road. On returning to the upstairs interior set, the cameras were already in place for the first take. A runner was asked to go to the next-door cottage, which was used as a temporary makeup and dressing area for the main cast. A few minutes later, Julie Walters, who played Mrs. Bumble, and David Ross, playing her husband, appeared. The first scene involved the two being in conversation whilst drinking tea in front of the window overlooking the workhouse yard. Renny Rye immediately observed a problem with the window ledge. In these traditional stone houses, the window ledges were often only eighteen inches high. The remedy was to have Julie Walters and David Ross kneeling on the floor with their cups of tea, while delivering their dialogue. It was a two-camera shot, one inside and simultaneously a second outside, focused up to the 'drawing room' window to capture the tea drinking moment. After two or three takes, Renny decided the scenes were fine. Observing the filming from my bedroom door, it was hilarious to watch Julie Walters suddenly keel over from her kneeling position to lay flat on her stomach, and roaring with laughter, exclaim: "What a bloody silly way to earn a living!"

When she had recovered and got up, I padded over and introduced myself. After a short dialogue, I could not possibly miss the opportunity to quip: "Oh, I can say I have had Julie Walters in my bedroom!" whilst vaguely waving my hands round at the room. Instantly she replied with a twinkle in her eye:

"You say that, and I sue!" We both laughed, but then she added:

"This is your home then?"

"Indeedy, it is."

"Perhaps, you would give me a quick tour then!"

Life can be so inexplicably surreal at times. One moment serving tourists cups of tea or coffee in my shop, and the next being adrift in the middle of a film location and chatting to another much-loved actress, whilst showing her round my home!

Later in the week, one particular scene stood out in my memory. It involved many support artists, who had to be herded into the workhouse yard and rained on by a water machine positioned a little way up Front Street. At the start of the scene, there was this distinct air of pantomime, which was frustrating the director. He was filming again from the interior upstairs drawing room, through the window, down to the bedraggled mob in the courtyard below. The takes just kept going, one after another. The crowd below us was getting wetter, and coupled with the chill of the snowy atmosphere, incredibly cold! The pantomime gaiety diffused into miserable silence and cheerless complaining, which was exactly what Renny Rye was trying to achieve. Finally, at 4pm, he was satisfied, and called it a wrap for the day. I have never seen the Butts empty so swiftly, as the poor frozen, and very wet support artists heard it was a wrap - in a split second, they were gone! A fitting end was Renny mentioning to a colleague that the cast indeed deserved extra pay for their terrific performance that day, and for the miserable time they had!

After the delightful visit with Joe, to watch Hayley in the 1992 production of "Fallen Angels", we settled into a comfortable, but slightly bohemian, routine. Joe would be moving to the Samuel Kings Secondary School in Alston after the summer holidays. After Joe's mum had taken off and we had moved into the town, the locals had been so supportive of our plight. In particular, a couple Gary and Denise, who lived quite close, used to have Joe and myself over for Sunday dinner, for which Joe was eternally grateful. After the meal, Denise, a fine pianist, would reach for her songbook and play random melodies. Gary, a guitarist and vocalist, would join in. It was so reminiscent of my childhood days, when as children, we would gather around the piano, as my mum would belt out songs from her songbook! Gary had long harboured the ambition to play in a band. The upshot was, these Sunday meals morphed into a Blues Band called CA9, named after Alston's postcode. The band went on to play until around 2009/2010. It consisted of Gary Alderson on rhythm guitar and vocals, his brother John on drums, an amazing blues and rock guitarist, Fraser Vincent, on lead guitar, replaced several years later when he relocated to Kent, by an equally brilliant guitarist named Tom Macmillan, and finally, yours truly on bass. We produced a recording in 1995 called "Cold Fever Blues", which proved popular. It was a brilliant experience, covering many venues across Cumbria and Northumbria.

I seriously enjoyed the humour of the band, especially being the outsider from Kent! Quite often, I would find myself at the butt end of some prank. One Saturday, we were busy setting the gear up in a venue. Although it was a reasonable size, the hall did not have a stage. The band had to fit into one corner, which could prove problematic, especially as we anticipated a large crowd. The various amplifiers were stacked to save floor space. John, the drummer yelled at me,

"Trev mate, go to the middle of the dance floor and jump up and down, to make sure the amps don't move."

This seemed a sensible suggestion, so I complied by going to the middle of the floor, and proceeded to jump up and down!

"Brilliant Trev, but any chance of jumping higher?

Again, by putting more vigour into the action, I managed to get higher.

"Fantastic Trev. But can you get your bloody back into it some more? I want it higher, much higher!"

Despite getting a trifle out of breath, and simply not observing the small crowd of bemused band members and staff, I managed to squeeze even more height! My exercise abruptly ended when Gary shouted at me,

"What are you bloody like Trev? You bloody idiot!" simultaneously waving his hand across his forehead in the time-honoured manner to indicate, I really was an idiot!

It wasn't until I stopped, the realisation dawned, I had been well and truly caught! This being confirmed by the number of hysterical people in the vicinity! Well, I thought it was a sensible suggestion!

9 AMAZING TIMES

The nineties saw an incredibly busy time for Hayley's theatre career. She wrote to me in the early part of 1993 to say "Fallen Angels", the play I had taken Joe to see in Billingham, was going to go on tour in Australia. Hayley had fallen in love with the country and looked forward to working there again. A major pleasure of doing the tour here in Britain was having her elder sister Juliet and Juliet's daughter Melissa with her. It was a great catchup time before Juliet and Melissa returned to New York, but they reunited again for the twelve week run of the show in Melbourne.

The following year, Hayley was back in the UK, and she was offered the role of the 'Countess of Chell' in the production of "The Card", based on the comedic novel bearing the same title, written by Arnold Bennett in 1911. The stage play was written as a collaboration between Keith Waterhouse and Willis Hall. It was presented as a musical, with the talented Tony Hatch writing the musical scores, coupled with Jackie Trent's lyrics. After the opening in London, at the Open Air Theatre in Regents Park, it went on a national tour. Very kindly, Hayley forwarded the nearest theatre details, which by coincidence was the Forum again in Billingham. My ticket was booked for the evening performance on the 5th November, a Saturday in 1994. Joe had already accepted an invite to a Guy Fawkes party and sleepover with his friend in the next village, which left me free to wander the roads again over the Pennine fells, to Billingham. The production itself was flawless, but it also gave me another 'first'! Hayley had one or two songs to deliver as part of the production. Apart from her "Let's Get Together" song in "The Parent Trap", I was never aware of her vocal talents. She has a fine voice. I made her chuckle backstage after the show. Having complimented her on her singing abilities, I regaled her with my anecdote of me not being a singer! Although having played in bands most of my life, it has to be said that the 'singing' in my head and the sounds that actually exit my mouth are not correlated in any shape or form! As I previously mentioned, the one and only time I ever sang on a stage was in 1960, at the age of fifteen, at a holiday adventure park, near Aberystwyth, mid Wales. Cliff Richard was enjoying his number one position in the top ten with "Living Doll", which I managed to murder, incredibly well indeed! Part of this anecdote was that a musical friend, who had been blessed with a fine voice, took me to task one day and said emphatically:

"Look Trevor, everyone can sing, your voice is a musical instrument and has to be regularly practised! Come round to mine and I will give you a singing lesson!"

I duly did as bid and landed on his doorstep for the lesson. He recorded me warbling through "Everyday", which was originally recorded by Buddy Holly. He proceeded to play it back, which I found to be excruciatingly embarrassing. He made a few suggestions for twenty minutes, or so, with each time making a fresh recording, to skilfully demonstrate how to strangle a song! He eventually announced he would put the kettle on, and it was wisely never mentioned again!

"You are not seriously saying you can't sing to that extent, are you?" Hayley asked, laughing.

"Probably worse, thinking about it." was my reply, but continued by asking, "The sound quality of the music was fantastic this evening. Were you singing along to a pre-recorded soundtrack? I couldn't see any band".

"No, there was a live band. Come on, I'll take you on stage, and I'll show you where they huddle!" I followed her through the maze of corridors until emerging onto the stage. She beckoned me to the stage right, and the scenery wing, and disappeared behind it. Hayley waved her arms around at this incredibly small space where the five members of the band had been ensconced for two hours to play their music! Huddled would be a fitting description, there was absolutely no room to swing the proverbial cat! It was amusing to see four of five wooden chairs with an upturned wooden box as the sitting area, and even more amusing to notice several lager cans, and empty glasses strewn around the cramped floor space!

We wandered back to Hayley's dressing room and sat chatting about family and general stuff. As usual, the time just flew by, with the theatre appearing much quieter as the background chatter of the cast and crew became increasingly inaudible. So suddenly, we heard the clicking of lights being turned off and a door being slammed shut! We were shut in!

"You stay here Trevor, I'll chase after the doorman, he won't have got far!" Hayley yelled over her shoulder at me as she dashed after him.

It felt a trifle odd, or even a tad surreal, sitting in a deserted theatre late in the evening. Fortunately, the light was still on in Hayley's dressing room, otherwise thoughts of the Phantom of the Opera might have overtaken my head, and

Hayley would have been presented with a demented wreck when she returned to collect me. She had caught up with him, and apparently, he was absolutely fine about it all. He assumed everyone had gone, especially the cast, who tend to be first out! He slammed the door for the second time, said his goodnight, and drove off into the night, leaving Hayley and myself in the car park.

"Come on Trevor, I'll walk you to your car", which she did. By chance, her own car was parked very close. We took our goodbyes, as we both drove off into the night and back into our entirely different lives. I just hoped Joe had an equally enjoyable evening with his friends at the bonfire and fireworks party. Again, something to look forward to when collecting him from his sleepover.

One of my favourite visits to Hayley's Hampton home was in the late eighties. It was, as I recall, a warm September afternoon, and the apple trees in her orchard bore testament to the kind weather. Hayley produced a bottle of wine, and we sat together on a double swing she had in the back garden. It was just a pleasant scenario, swinging gently backwards and forwards, sipping wine. The chat freely moved to families, in particular her two boys, Crispian and Jason, and my Joe. Part of being a parent was wondering what path your offspring would take. As mentioned before, Crispian ended up in 1996, being lead vocalist and lead guitarist in an incredibly popular band known as Kula Shaker, which resonated the eastern cultural, psychedelic sound. He later became a film writer and producer in the twenty first century, making the iconic horror, comedy "The Fear of Everything", in 2012, with Simon Pegg in the lead role. Crispian's half-brother, known as Jason Lawson, as his father, Leigh Lawson, had adopted him, had a successful career as a theatre director.

Joe, on the other hand, found his destiny lay with figures,

numbers, and spreadsheets. He is invited into companies, alongside like-minded executives, usually by investors, to improve economic production using statistical analysis to facilitate a strategic management plan. However, he is also a talented pianist and guitarist, but had no interest in developing any stage skills! Having said this, I always look forward to jam sessions alongside Joe.

These are the things Hayley and I discussed at great length, gently swinging to and fro in the September sunshine, sipping the wine and generally being relaxed. The next stage in our world would be to ponder the possibilities of grandchildren at some point in the future!

As it transpired, the visit to see Hayley perform in "The Card" would be my last until she played 'Margaret' in "Dead Guilty", which ran from July 1995 to March 1996, at the Apollo theatre, in the famous Shaftesbury Avenue, sometimes dubbed the theatre mile in London. Starring alongside Hayley was Jenny Seagrove. The play was a gripping thriller, with twists and turns throughout, penned by Richard Harris and directed by Auriol Smith. Contrary to some critical reviews, I thoroughly enjoyed the performance, and of course it is the customer who is always right!

While Hayley faced all sorts of dark deeds in the play, it gave me a sharp recall to serious events that overtook me in 1968.

Back then, I had started my garage in Sandgate, a small coastal village between Folkestone and Hythe, in Kent. At lunchtime, I would walk the short distance into the village to sit and enjoy a bite to eat, read the paper and chat with an extremely affable cafe proprietor. However, this cafe was closed on a Tuesday, so I would walk an extra one hundred yards to a second cafe, where the elderly lady who ran the establishment was not so communicative! You would be met with an abrupt:

"YES?"

Invariably, this cafe would be empty, as indeed it was on this occasion. My order of a cheese and tomato roll accompanied by a cup of tea would duly arrive in dead silence. I would accept this with good grace and receive a grunt in return. The only sound was the ticking of the wall clock and the hum of an ancient refrigerator coming from the direction of the counter. Having finished my snack, and glancing at the clock, which reminded me it was two o'clock, I went to the counter, paid my dues, and left with a smile, which was ignored.

The weather was pleasantly warm as I returned to the crash repair workshop to continue repairing a Morris Minor with a rather sad dent in its front wing. Somewhere around five pm, I shut up shop and started my two mile walk back home to Folkestone. Being coastal presented the option to either walk the seafront promenade, or follow the main road back past the two cafes in the High Street. I chose the latter, which would confirm the old adage, 'wrong place at the wrong time'!

On approaching the cafe where I had sat earlier, I noticed a roadblock was in place to stop the traffic, with two or three policemen stopping pedestrians on the pavement. Obviously, something was afoot! On reaching the policemen, they stopped me to inquire whether I ever used the cafe directly beside us. Truthfully, I answered yes, adding I had only been in there that day to have lunch, leaving at two pm. Well, that was it!

Within seconds, I found myself in a police car being taken to the Folkestone Police Station at high speed, to face relentless interrogation, as the elderly woman was murdered at approximately two pm! Strangled actually. Though not the kindest of souls, she did not deserve to perish in such a manner.

The fact that I was young at the time, being twenty-three, and just starting out in the business world, coupled with evidence that money had been stolen from the till, indicating the motive, convinced the police I had, without doubt, committed the heinous crime. The questioning was incessantly repetitive, with the police encouraging me to confess and get it off my chest! It all seemed so surreal to me, one moment eating cheese and tomato rolls, the next being accused of murder! Fortunately for me, the situation was resolved at about eleven pm that evening. After another session of probing questions, the police broke off for a coffee break. Ten minutes later, one of the officers reappeared with a mug of coffee for me, but added:

"There you are son, after you have had your drink, you are free to leave. I believe your mum and dad are still in the waiting room."

"I'm free to go?"

"Yes"

"How, why?" My mind was racing. Was this some sort of softening up technique, so I would drop my guard and incriminate myself in some way?

The answers to my niggling questions were swiftly explained by the officer, that a retired doctor, who lived in the Norfolk Hotel, dead opposite the cafe where the elderly lady had so cruelly died, had committed suicide that evening, leaving a note admitting his terrible crime. It is thought the doctor and the deceased woman had been in some relationship, which, for whatever reason, went horribly wrong. The oddity was the money taken from the till. The doctor was comfortably off, so the money issue did not stack up as a motive. Unfortunately, there was another depressing reason for the theft, with a dreadful indictment of the human condition. Shortly after my departure from the cafe that fateful day, the doctor had crept into the cafe via the back door and committed the crime and left. A short time later, a van driver called into the cafe to make a delivery, observed the chaos, saw the till open, scooped out the money, and used the cafe telephone to contact the police to raise the alarm. After questioning, the driver confessed to this callous act, and richly deserved the custodial sentence for his efforts to make a few quid!

After the show "Dead Guilty", closed in March 1996, Hayley was invited to join the cast for a reprisal of her portrayal of 'Anna' in the "King and I", on a planned extensive tour of the U.S.A. beginning in 1997, finishing in 1998. This proved to be a pivotal moment in her life. Fellow actor Firdous Bamji, who was her lead co-star as the King of Siam, also became her leading man in her personal life. They have been together ever since. Firdous is an absolutely charming man, who I met after being invited backstage at the Cambridge Arts Theatre in 2012, when Hayley appeared in "Ladies in Lavender". Firdous was born in Mumbai, India, where he spent his education at the Kodaikanal International School, in the southern part of the country, before completing at the University of North Carolina at Greensboro and the University of South Carolina, where he obtained a bachelor's degree in Journalism and a master's in Fine Art. While completing his masters, he became engrossed in the theatre arts, making appearances in roles such as Eric Bogosian's "Suburbia". He gained much critical acclaim for his various roles, resulting in a busy work schedule, touring with productions around the USA. gaining public popularity as he went. Firdous was no stranger to the touring world when he joined Hayley for their American tour.

Very kindly, Hayley forwarded a copy of the tour dates, listing the hotels allocated to the cast, and the miles between venues. Some distances were staggering! For example,

Nashville, Tennessee to Boston, Massachusetts 1098 miles! It gives an idea of the hectic life an actor leads, as the same would apply to the whole production company. The sheer logistics of moving the stage sets, the costumes, the props from city to city, and then reassembling the stage sets, ready for the next opening night! Some of the venues were for just a week's run, such as the Fox Theatre in Atlanta, Georgia, whilst others extended to three weeks, as did the performances at the Wang Centre in Boston, which would ease the travelling pressure.

While Hayley was touring the States with "The King and I", I experienced a totally unexpected sea adventure with my chum Tone.

Sadly, he had lost the love of life Jackie, in 1995, to cancer. She was a beautiful lady, with a great sense of humour and a wonderful soft, West Country accent, being of Plymouth origin. They had met when, as a young man, Tone was sent to the Plymouth Naval College to complete his officer's course. Jackie was a sixth form student at the local girls' grammar school. She used to shin down a tree by her bedroom window, to go out on a date with Tone, instead of getting homework done! Clearly, it did not affect her education, as she became a school teacher herself. Tone's naval career took him around the world. For several years, they settled in New Zealand, where he was, for a time, an officer on the ferries that plied between the two islands. Eventually, they moved back to the UK, and he worked on the cross-channel ferries from Dover, hence his connection with the Zeebrugge disaster in the eighties. While we were still living in Kent, he would occasionally telephone to ask (as if I needed asking):

"Hi Wrighty, do you fancy a trip over to Zeebrugge today, my old cobber?", using his most eloquent Australian accent! "I can promise yer some chocolate eclairs and mugs of coffee", he would add, knowing full well that it would be the clincher!

"Right on Bruce!" I would reply in my poor interpretation of an Australian accent!

I will freely admit, I enjoyed these hikes across the channel, especially being allowed on the bridge. Captain Cook had nothing on me, as I regularly discovered Zeebrugge!

The captain must be on the bridge for arriving at a port, and for disembarking. On one occasion, as we entered Zeebrugge Harbour, Tone, alongside the first, and second, officers, were being very professional by being on standby to dock, when one of the officers yelled,

"Cor, come and look at this!" We all took a closer look through the screen, observing the bow, where an unfortunate young lady was put at the mercy of the sea breeze, with her dress firmly round her head!

In 1996, Tone and his new lady friend had purchased a beautiful schooner called 'Narooma' and decided to sail across the planet to New Zealand. They estimated they would be gone for about three years, but in the event, the trip lasted two days in the summer 1998! Joe and I had gone to Kent to wave them off from the Dover marina, where 'Narooma' was moored under the shadow of the iconic Dover Castle. Joe's mum and her husband had joined us to wave the couple farewell, as they disappeared west, into the setting sun. We returned to Cumbria the following day, only to receive a call from Tone saying they had got to Brighton okay, and moored. After celebrating with a glass or three, Tone's lady friend, Camilla, decided to pay her respects to the marina toilet, missed her footing on some steps and broke a leg in two places! The around the world sailing trip was inevitably postponed for Camilla's leg to repair. Their plan B would therefore be instigated. Go and live in their house in Spain, which they had acquired a year or two earlier. 'Narooma' would have to be moved down to the south of Spain. By August 1998, I had set up a cabinet making business producing bespoke furniture in a local factory, while a lady friend took care of the teashop and craft centre in the town centre. Without warning, one day Tone strode through the workshop door, and with his usual grin he got straight to the point by posing the question:

"Hey Wrighty, fancy sailing my boat down to a marina in the south of Spain, from Brighton?"

This was a tough one. After careful deliberation, which took all of three seconds, I answered in the affirmative!

Obviously, I ran this past Joe, who by then was sixteen and had just left Samuel Kings School, and he was totally cool with it. A week later, the three of us, Tone, me and Terry, who was a fellow skipper on the ferries in the 80's, at the time of the Zeebrugge disaster, arrived at the Brighton marina where 'Narooma' was moored. Terry had, in fact, been given the brief to take over the stricken 'Herald of Free Enterprise' from the serving captain David Lewry, who survived after it had capsized in the English Channel with great loss of life. Terry gave evidence at the resulting inquest and enquiry.

The Brighton Marina lies under the shadow of the famous Roedean private school for girls. We had arrived late in the afternoon, which gave us time to relax and draw up plans. We would share the watch by taking an eight hour shift each, to keep 'Narooma' going twenty-four hours.

"You realise, I have no practical experience at sailing?"

"You'll be fine Wrighty!"

Tony and Terry had been poring over the charts, whilst I got accustomed to the washing up area in the galley. 'Narooma' was not only architecturally pleasing to the eye, but also incredibly functional. The galley had an amazing cooker where saucepans had a slot area fitment which coped with any sea movement. All culinary items had their place. At sea, it is not good to have items flying all round the galley. However, I was amused at the shower unit. Fine in a marina, but an interesting experience at sea trying to keep under the shower! There was a similar problem with the urinal, it paid to sit down to spend a penny, whilst at sea!

My cabin was at 'the pointy end', as Tone would explain it. Terry and Tone shared the two double cabins in the aft or blunt end of the vessel. Narooma was a fine, spacious vessel. She sported three masts and, should the wind drop, she could travel under her Perkins diesel internal engine. The main saloon was incredibly comfortable, with a selection of built-in settees around the circumference of the seating area, and a fixed table at one end, close to the steps leading down to the galley. My cabin was forward from the galley on the lower level, which doubled as the food storage area. Laying on my bunk, I could look up at the cabin ceiling, staring through the toughened plastic skylight, to observe the outside, which was a little worrying, especially watching the odd rogue wave wash across the deck above me!

Tone said we would make an early start the following morning, from the marina, to catch the morning tide. There was a copious amount of alcohol consumed to ensure the glasses worked, before retiring to bed! Next day at the start of the adventure, Tone had cooked a great breakfast, and afterwards I was reintroduced to the tea towel! The weather was brilliant. My two shipmates did last minute checks and untied the mooring ropes before starting the engine, which immediately burst into responsive life. The vessel had the option to be steered, either internally or externally. As we enjoyed the early morning sun, Tone gently edged 'Narooma' out from her berth and into the marina centre channel leading through to the open English Channel.

"Okay, Captain Wrighty, it's your turn! You take her out to sea matey! Simple really, see that green light, keep it on your left, you'll be fine! Just try not to bump the other boats, their owners can get a tad sniffy if you do!"

"What? Where are you two going?" I asked watching them disappear down into the cabin, whilst trying to suppress my growing anxiety, or to be more honest, sheer terror!

"I'm off to have a pee and Terry will get some coffee, won't be a tick!"

And they were gone! There was me, totally inexperienced, steering a fifty-four foot, twenty ton vessel out of the Brighton marina, desperately trying to avoid colliding with any other moored boats! The pointy end seemed such a long way ahead of me! I quickly became aware of not oversteering, to prevent the otherwise unavoidable zig zag pattern developing in the wash of the boat. Less was indeed more! Following the green lights as instructed, I could observe the sea ahead.

To that point, it was all plain sailing, in the manner of speaking, but the moment we left the calm of the marina and hit the open sea, it all dramatically changed! I had trouble keeping my rear end on the seat whilst trying to hang on to the steering wheel. The sea was slightly choppy! At this point, Tone and Terry reappeared on deck, and inexplicably, Tone started rolling and lighting a cigarette, and Terry produced three mugs of coffee without spilling a drop!

"Second job for you, third officer Trev," said Terry amicably, adding: "Here take the tray and mugs, see if you can do another brew, and get them back up here, without spilling a drop."

Unknown to me, my two shipmates had planned this initiation to see whether I would cope with sailing. If I had failed, they would have returned me to shore! Fortunately, I passed the test, even though I only managed to get back up from the galley with a mouth full of coffee! The course was set to sail west, following the English coastline, with our destination being Falmouth in Cornwall, where we moored in the local marina, strolled up to the local supermarket and loaded up with the necessary extensive alcohol provisions, plus a few essential food supplies. As with the previous evening, we enjoyed one over the eight, one for the hair of the dog, one for the left ear of the dog, indeed one for the right ear of the dog! Of course, I lulled the brain into a sense of wellbeing and sleep. The next day, I woke to the aromas of cooking drifting in from the adjacent galley, where Tone was busy putting the breakfast together. As it was a beautiful August morning, the three of us clambered out onto the deck, carrying our trays and enjoying our breakfast, watching the seagulls, who were hovering close by just in case we dropped any titbits. The strong morning sun soon dispelled the light sea mist, as Tone and Terry started their boat checks, before starting the engine and nosing our way back into the sea. In the meantime, I had reintroduced myself to the tea towel again! Tone had set the course to travel south, not only across the English Channel, but also the notorious Bay of Biscay, whose fickle temperament was well known to the sailing fraternity and even to the big cruisers, ferries and oil tankers. Eighty foot waves were not uncommon!

I was allocated the first watch, from eight am to noon, and the second, eight pm to midnight. Terry was allocated the midday to four pm and midnight to four am, with Captain Tone doing the four to eight in the am and four to eight pm. There was one golden rule to follow; the relieving watch would make a cup of coffee for the person coming off watch! Each watch would be armed with a flask of coffee before going on duty, as it was deemed, a tad dangerous to leave the steering area, especially at night, to make coffee in the galley! It is a whole new ball game, from running along the coastline, to experiencing the navigation required to cross one of the busiest sea routes in the world. Captain Tone gave me preliminary lessons in use of the radar at the three and twelve mile scan readings. He also showed me how to read the direction a ship was travelling at night, by which light you could see; green port and red starboard. Our destination was La Coruna, on the northwest point of Spain, about 440 nautical miles. The Captain showed me how to plot the course by using ruler, pencil and compass, to work out, taking into account prevailing winds and currents, the time of arrival. I found this an amazing skill to possess. Although 'Narooma' had a built-in GPS system, Captain Tone would always have his trusted sextant by him, as he would say, and I quote:

"Water and electricity do not make good bedfellows!"

Tone's only disappointment with the crossing was that wind never picked up sufficiently to justify the sails being unfurled. Nevertheless, it was blissfully enjoyable chugging to the steady rhythm of the Perkins diesel engine and watching the passing traffic! The weather was perfect, so we spent much time on the deck, with 'Narooma' being steered from the stern. I found it fascinating watching the dolphins race and play with the 'pointy end' of the yacht. The evenings would be spent on deck having a drink or three until the sunset, and we would then retreat down into the salon where the internal steering wheel could be engaged. Tone would check the map readings to make sure we were on course, and, rightly, he would peer out of the salon's port holes in all directions to make sure I had not missed any shipping on the radar, or visibly out of the forward screen! I must admit to being a trifle apprehensive left in control of 'Narooma' on my first proper watch, but incredibly excited! As they turned in, Tone made it clear, if I was not sure of anything, whatever the potential problem, to wake him immediately! At midnight, Terry turned up, made a coffee, and joined me at the watch position. Although the shift started at eight pm, I was just two hours on my own, which I suspect was planned that way, since I had no experience of sailing! In the event, it had been a quiet shift. After a short exchange of pleasantries, I retired down to my forward bunk and fell asleep to the sound of waves slapping against the hull and watching the moon and stars through the hatch. After what seemed a few minutes, there was a tap on the door, and Tone's voice ringing out:

"Rise and shine Wrighty. Coffee needs brewing! "

Looked at the watch. 7.45am, oh my word, I'm going to be late for my watch! And of course, I needed to get the coffee too. Threw on clothes, opened the cabin door, was met with the delicious aroma of fresh brewed coffee, plus a pile of bacon butties! What a treat! Again, the sun shone and the 'Narooma' was still chugging her way towards the Spanish coast, as she had been obligingly doing all night whilst I slumbered. After breakfast, when everything was washed and stowed away, I took my position again on watch, whilst Tone and Terry attended odd jobs around the boat. This was our third day from Falmouth, and land should come into view, and sure enough, it did. The horizon seemed to take on a thicker edge, which became jagged in appearance as we slowly crept nearer. Checking with the binoculars, I was indeed viewing the Cantabrian Mountain range of north Spain.

"Land Ahoy Captain", I yelled loudly. This was a cherished moment, I wanted to shout since starting the watch! Tone sauntered over, peered through the screen and confirmed the sighting of land.

"Yep, that's land ahead alright. Still got a couple of hours before reaching La Coruna, so I have another little job for you Wrighty. The green light has gone out on the pointy end. Would you like to get along there and replace the bulb please? Quite straightforward. Take the lens off, replace the bulb with a new one, and screw the lens back on. Simples, really! While you are doing that, I'll take over the watch and Terry will make three coffees."

"Nay problem, El Capitan", I replied, taking the screwdriver and replacement bulb from him. Cheerfully, I climbed the steps to the exterior deck and manoeuvred towards the pointy end of 'Narooma'. The sea was a little choppy, so I found it easier to go along the length of the yacht on hands and knees, as the safety rail was only about fifteen inches high, and it would negate the possibility of shouting "Man overboard"! After a somewhat turbulent few minutes, I succeeded to reach the pointy end. The problem was, of course, the sea was coming over the bow, with 'Narooma' dipping and rising from the water! It seemed to take hours to gradually remove the three lens screws, with the constant fear that the screwdriver, lens, bulb and I would disappear over the side, at any time soon! I had my arm around the bow to steady myself, constantly lowering my head to take the next wave! Eventually, I managed to replace the lens without loss of anything. I triumphantly, but carefully turning around, still on my hands and knees, to start my perilous journey back. I glanced into the cabin, where both Tone and Terry had descended into some demented hysteria. Dripping wet, I finally climbed back into the sanctuary of the salon, gleefully holding out the screwdriver and spent bulb. Trying to keep a straight face, the El Capitan made the observation:

"Well, bloody done Wrighty! Good one! We are both impressed, here matey, have a mug of coffee, and oh, by the way, personally I would have waited until we got to the marina!!!!!" At which point they both collapsed back into their tormented hysterics!

"Bastards!" I uttered as the proverbial penny dropped. We put our tourist hats on after we docked in La Coruna later that morning, and enjoyed visiting the old Cathedral and sixteenth century Castle. As we approached the coastline, the famous Roman lighthouse, known as the Tower of Hercules, came into view, which has been protecting shipping since the second century!

This area is the site of the old city, which had a turbulent history, with the Vikings constantly attacking during the ninth and tenth centuries. Later on, the area saw the famous battle where the British under Sir John Moore were defending the Spanish from the invading Napoleon Bonaparte, and his French troops. History notes Sir John Moore is buried there. While we visited the old city, we had a few moments in the sixteenth century castle, which had played a part in the defence of the city. Interestingly, my first primary school was named the Sir John Moore's Primary School in my home garrison town of Folkestone.

With the notion of taking the weight off our feet and quenching our thirst, we drifted back towards the marina, and took a respite in one of the many outdoor cafes, before returning to 'Narooma' via dinghy. The marina was so busy, there were no vacant moorings, and consequently we had moored and dropped anchor just outside the harbour.

"Best check the fuel to the outboard is switched on, El Capitan." I teased Tone.

"And you can shut it," came the reply.

The reason I mentioned this outboard fuel tap, was that on the incoming trip from 'Narooma' to shore, Tone had lost a little street cred, or rather 'sea cred', given the situation. We had lowered the dinghy from the davit into the sea, and we three clambered in. El Capitano tugged on the starter pulley without anything happening. This he repeated, over and over again, with the same lack of success. The language was getting a tad blue! I offered my limited experience and expertise, by suggesting:

"Have you made sure the fuel tap is switched on?"

"Of course I have switched the bloody fuel tap on!" came the terse reply, as again, he desperately tugged on the pulley without success. He fumbled with the fuel tap.

"Of course, I have NOT switched the bloody fuel tap on!!!"

The outboard burst into life and, with a rattled El Capitan at the helm, we shot across the outer harbour to shore at fifty million miles an hour, drenching us on the way. However, we soon dried out in the Spanish sun after landing on the quayside.

Tone cooked a delicious, evening meal, and we settled into the familiar routine of toasting everything, from the sun over the yardarm to the dolphins.

We caught the morning tide and set sail south towards Portugal. Our next destination was a quaint old coastal town called Peniche, 379 nautical miles down the Portuguese coast. Tone, having studied the maps, charted the course, keeping a safe one mile distance from the mountainous shoreline, the danger being any rocky shelves below the waves. The journey was spectacular, to say the least. The wind was light, so Tone again shared his disappointment about chugging under the engine, rather than using wind power. After the obligatory intoxication and storytelling, I took up my watch position, while the other two continued to chat. Somewhere near 11 pm, I observed a magical sight I had never witnessed before. Directly in front of 'Narooma', the surface of the sea was lit up by an eerie, fluorescent green light, which seemed to go in all directions! For one dramatic moment, I thought I had steered into a series of submarines on some night manoeuvres!

"El Capitan, we have a situation here, please attend the bridge!" Which in this case meant get off the settee and take the half a dozen steps to the watch station! The Captain observed this amazing display, and laughed, before explaining it was a large shoal of the infamous Portuguese man of war jellyfish that gave off this eerie light, which attracted smaller fish and plankton, on which they fed. He added:

"Please don't go out and fall overboard, as they give a nasty nip, and I am not prepared to bloody dive in and save you!"

"Good point, well made!" was the only response I could muster!

The next day, we continued our journey south, following the Portuguese coastline. The wind had picked up sufficiently to sail under canvas. Terry was a master skipper in sailing. He had taught cadets this historic art at many naval colleges during his career at sea. Basically, my job was to listen and obey! Winding the sails up the three masts when asked to do so, getting the various boom masts operational, making sure all ropes were correctly stowed away, to prevent tripping over, as the vessel would dramatically tilt as the wind filled into her sails! Terry organised these procedures to make a smooth transition from switching the motor off and adjusting the various booms to move and scoop the wind up in the sails. Done correctly, the vessel gently takes up the sailing, tilted position, where the only noise, apart from the wind, is the slapping of water against the hull. What an experience! For purely safety reasons, Tone had taken 'Narooma' a few miles further out to sea, as any 'tacking' could bring the vessel dangerously close to the shoreline rock outcrops. Tone learned a lot from having Terry with us. Although he was a skipper, he did not possess the sailing knowledge his old friend had. Terry demonstrated on several occasions, by only using the sails, he had 'Narooma' held stationary in the sea, not unlike holding a car just by using the clutch on a hill. Several miles before reaching Peniche, the sails were furled and stowed again, as with the other equipment. With a turn of the key, the Perkins motor burst into life again, and settled into a dependable rhythmic chug as we nosed our way forward to the very old town of Peniche, overshadowed by its ancient, now semi derelict, Moorish Castle, ravaged by the Atlantic storms, whilst defending the town from possible invaders.

We had just moored in the small quayside, when two gruff armed policemen drove up, leapt from their vehicle, and jumped on board 'Narooma'! They were attached to the Portuguese coast guard and checking craft passing through their national water, especially if they landed ashore. Earlier in the day, I had taken a photograph of a light plane that appeared to be shadowing and circling us. We assumed this was a follow up visit, to safeguard against possible drug smuggling. In the event, the guards went through the vessel, prodding and poking and opening various cupboards. Finally, they decided we were not part of some drug cartel, and after checking our passports, said it was okay to stay for a night. As evening was drawing on, we decided to relax, have a meal on the deck in the evening sun, and watch the shadow of the castle gradually spread longer as the sunset progressed. Needless to say, we were aided and abetted in our relaxation by one or three alcoholic beverages that drifted our way! The need for a watch was not necessary, given we were in dock for the night. Must confess to having a great night's sleep, aided by the gentle motion of the boat, plus the soporific splashing of the sea against the hull.

Next morning, we rose at a sensible time, instead of silly o'clock, and enjoyed another one of Tone's culinary delights, sitting out in the morning sun. The big plus being in the harbour, was having a shower without ducking and diving, trying to keep your body under the water! Ablution completed, we rambled at leisure the short distance to the old part of Peniche, passing through a small harbour designated for local fishermen to continue their historic way of life, farming the sea. Directly behind was the impressive ruins of the castle, so imposing in the early morning sun. Arriving at the heart of old town Peniche, we were greeted by an elderly man perched on a stool and finger-picking his guitar. Locals were going about their business, setting up stalls and opening shops for the coming day of tourists flocking to the town in cars and coaches from the nearby 1P6 route. Peniche was renowned for its beaches and surfing, especially having an Atlantic coastline, where the conditions were perfect for the long dramatic rolling ride on the surfboard. What encapsulated the atmosphere of Peniche was two elderly women busy cooking fresh caught fish on the pavement. After cleaning the pavement, olive oil was spread evenly over the surface, leaving it for a few minutes as the sun got to work, and then the prepared fish would be laid out to cook. The three of us thought the same thing. We will have a local coffee, buy some of these aromatic fish, escort them back to 'Narooma' and devour them with salad and wine! We stayed the rest of the day, watching the high rollers on their surfboards and generally soaking up the ambience of this old principality.

What a difference a few hours can make! We were rudely awoken the next morning, by 'Narooma' desperately trying to break free from her mooring. The wind had blown in from the Atlantic and had a great influence on us. Tone and Terry had hopped ashore to tighten the mooring ropes, which helped by taking the slack up, and seemed to pacify 'Narooma' and prevent her running away. It was going to be a very bumpy ride indeed! Our breakfast was spent in the salon, using damp tea towels as place mats for the first time on this voyage, mainly to keep the plates from sliding to the floor. It was considered sensible to grip your plate as an added precaution! After breakfast, I went down to the galley to wash up and stow away the utensils. While I was engrossed with these chores, El Capitan and Terry had made the usual checks, started the 'Narooma's' engine, untied the mooring ropes and headed the pointy end towards the awaiting, somewhat choppy Atlantic Ocean! Suddenly, I lurched from side to side, as the yacht hit the open water. The only way to maintain any useful position was to wedge myself between the galley kitchen units! Fortunately, the cups, plates and bowls were all plastic, which was just as well, as several of these items ended up on the floor, trying to frantically copy youngsters dancing at some rock festival. The refrigerator door in the meantime was wildly flapping in a demented fashion, refusing point blank to close.

Climbing up the steps to the salon and trying to circumvent the furniture also presented a few problems. We were now in the Atlantic. The pointy end was dipping into the waves, which rushed over the hull and covered the forward screen, before receding back into the swirling tide. 'Narooma' had the same motion as a rocking horse, with the added benefit of a sideward roll! After trying to join the other two on deck, I was met by a rather windswept and soaked Terry, who said it would be safer to steer from inside, which he did by taking up the normal watch position, which allowed Tone to retreat to the relative safety of the salon. Despite knowing my crewmates had spent their entire lives at sea, I still found it amazing how they seemed to suddenly have pistons rather than legs! They carried on, in a perfectly normal fashion, as though all was flat and calm!

"Time for coffee, Wrighty!" Tone exclaimed with a smile spreading across his weatherbeaten, face. He must have seen the groan in my head as he added "No problem, I fancy a mug of coffee, not a dribble, I'll make it", which he did. He frustratedly got all three mugs up from the galley without spilling a single bloody drop!

We rock'n'rolled our way due south, following the Portuguese coast, as Tone had decided it would be prudent to proceed using the engine rather than the sails, in such strong winds. That evening, as previously, we ate our meal, grasping the plate stuck to the damp tea towel. A bowl of soup would be totally out of the question! Strangely enough, we still managed to drink a toast to 'Narooma', the seagulls who doggedly followed us, the dolphins who swam beside us, and the sinking sun!

I had a bit of a disaster, on completing my watch, and disappearing to my cabin just after midnight. Got into my bunk and fell asleep immediately. What I had not noticed was that a catering size jar of maple syrup had rolled off the shelf and rested on the pillow close to my head. The next morning, when I woke up to start my morning watch, I found to my dismay, the pillow had stuck to my head! If it didn't make my day, it certainly did for my fellow crewmates! They just fell about laughing hysterically at this apparition standing in front of them in shorts and T-shirts, with a pink and white striped pillow glued with syrup to his head!

We arrived down by the Portuguese Algarve, where we would normally steer east across the Cadiz Bay, going towards Gibraltar and the Mediterranean Sea, but Captain Tone fancied dropping further south, to get the experience of the Atlantic. This we did for some hours. And what an experience too. The waves were no longer choppy, but became massive rolling hills, which picked 'Narooma' up as though she was just a matchbox. One minute riding high on the crest of a hill, and the next moment going headlong into a deep trough of water. Obviously, we remained in the salon through this phase of the journey, as a fair bit of seawater was washing over the boat. Then it happened! A rogue wave doubled up on the preceding wave, and poor old 'Narooma' took the impact on the starboard. We lurched over to such an extent that I was looking down at Tone and Terry, who were now on their backs laying on the portside, as I desperately clung on, to prevent myself from falling across the salon floor to join them! The light in the salon went a strange greeny, grey as the wave washed over the top of us! El Capitan merely grinned at my anguished face and added:

"Nay worries shipmate, she will come upright!" "Narooma" proved them right and returned to her upright position. Tone thought we had had enough excitement for one day, and we should change our course to aim for Gibraltar. By the time we were back in Cadiz Bay, the weather had subsided, the sea was reasonably tranquil, with the clouds giving way to a perfect late afternoon clear blue-sky and sun.

The rock of Gibraltar is incredibly impressive on the approach route, rising so dramatically to its 426 metre peak. It was still light when we docked at the incredibly busy marina, so busy we had to moor alongside another vessel, as there weren't any vacant berths. Traditionally, by doing this, you had a right of way across the next vessel to get to the quayside, though of course, it was a polite courtesy to call out before encroaching on someone else's boat! Gibraltar is not just home to a tourist industry, it is an important shipping point for the vessels traversing the globe, and of course a strategically important military base for the Royal Navy.

We had only just tied up before a booming voice came across a public address system,

"Would the Skipper and any crew aboard 'Narooma' please attend the Customs area with their passports, please?"

El Capitan said under his breath, something to the effect, we will when we have had a cuppa!

"Would the Skipper and crew of 'Narooma' report to Customs NOW?"

"I think we had better go before they come to us! "said a grinning El Capitano. Armed with passports, we clambered across the adjacent vessel, climbed the metal steps onto the quayside, and made our way over to the Customs area. After the checks, we wandered into the main town. It had a distinct colonial atmosphere reflecting a bygone era, especially the British Consulate building, with its whitewashed walls highlighting the Victorian timber filigree, and complete with an enclosed walled garden, abundantly full of orange and palm trees. We sat outside a cafe close by, drinking our coffee, and soaking up the wonderful evening ambience. The three of us unanimously agreed we would stay another day to play and do the tourist bit, rather than cast off in the morning and miss out exploring this island jewel.

The following morning, having swapped mooring places with the vessel moored alongside, we waved goodbye to our marina neighbours as they set sail on their voyage across the Atlantic. We lazily ambled in the morning sun, back into the town, and called a taxi that would take us to the top of the rock. Sadly, the chairlift was not open that particular day, which was a shame, as we missed a spectacular way to the top. The driver was obviously au fait with the road, as he slung the taxi into the bends at breakneck speed! He seemed fairly oblivious to other road users, as he steered one handed, whilst sunbathing his other arm out of the window. The views from the summit were stunning. On one hand, a perfect vista of the Mediterranean Sea and the Spanish coast, plus the added bonus of the North African mountainous coastline on the horizon, and, by turning round, a splendid view of the airport, which separates the United Kingdom from Spain. It was fascinating to watch the traffic stop to allow the incoming flights and departures. The only route into Gibraltar from mainland Spain was via this one road crossing the runway, with the added problem of border control and custom checks! While we enjoyed the view, our demented taxi driver tried to stop one of the resident Barbary apes from ripping his felt roof and breaking the window wipers!

The descent in the taxi was no less fraught, as we hurtled down the steep, narrow winding road to the amazing concert cavern below the summit. This naturally formed cavern is the home of many orchestras that perform in this unique setting. The acoustic quality of this underground theatre is totally amazing! Our taxi driver tour guide explained that Napoleon Bonaparte, during his quest to dominate Europe, had dug many tunnels into Gibraltar Rock to reinforce his strategically defensive position at the entrance to the Mediterranean Sea. The guide had also explained that Gibraltar Rock had a flat face on the eastern wall, to collect rainwater for the benefit of the thirtythree thousand local population. It also had giant desalination units to purify the seawater. I'm pretty sure the taxi driver was desperate to get back to his base and do another party before the evening started to draw in. We were propelled at an alarming speed down the winding road, with a quick view of the naval base and marina. One more stop was made at an ice cream vendor, where we gratefully slurped ice cream cornets down our fairly parched throats, before we finally arrived at the taxi office. We paid and tipped the driver, thanking him for the informative tour, but he had already turned to gather another group of tourists to hurtle up to the summit!

We sauntered through the narrow streets, stopping to peer at some piece of Spanish architecture or British Colonial style residence, before finally arriving back at the marina and 'Narooma'.

The evening meal was served, again on deck, in the warmth of the magnificent sunset. A flamenco guitarist could be heard in the distance, adding to the ambience. Of course, the addition of much alcohol enhanced the evening somewhat! While we sat enjoying the evening, we wondered whether the taxi driver was still desperately struggling with a Barbary ape on the summit of the rock, or hurtling up and down at breakneck speed, trying to get one more group in before sunset!

I actually don't remember going to bed, but must have, as the first thing I knew, the sun was streaming down through the hatch. It was a combination of fresh sea air, walking, fine food and a tad too much local wine!

Breakfast finished, we made our way to cast off and chug out of the marina, leaving Gibraltar gradually disappearing behind us. As we travelled eastbound past Gibraltar, the water collecting flat face became visible. It was much larger than I imagined, but then there were several thousand throats to quench!

The wind was light, but sufficient enough to fill the sails, which were duly unfurled. With the engine turned off, we proceeded in our new askew angle! We had ventured away from the Spanish coastline to get a closer look at the North African continent. The first view of the coast was the magnificent Atlas Mountains, which run along the northern edge of Africa. In the sunlight, they had this wonderful, bluish tinge which seemed to gently move in the growing heat! Having enjoyed this vista, we turned and tacked back under sail towards the Spanish mainland, and ended up in Cala Del Perro, a quiet bay a few miles from our final destination at Marina Del Este. We dropped anchor and furled the sails away, before settling down to our final night on 'Narooma'. Although, of course, I wanted to return to regale Joe with our various adventures, there was a degree of sadness that the experience of this life at sea would end the following day. These feelings were quickly numbed by the normal intake of alcohol and another fine meal cooked by El Capitano. I suspect my shipmates were also having regrets about leaving 'Narooma', as the drinking spree was conducted in a much more subdued fashion. Again, getting to sleep that night was no problem, when the sun disappeared below the horizon.

The darkness engulfed us, with the Spanish coastline lit up by street lamps and moving vehicle headlamps. The surrounding mountains became covered in twinkling lights as their inhabitants switched the power on. It was a perfect way to end this boating experience.

The following morning, Tone thought that as we had about three hours to motor to Marina Del Este, we would take an hour each. I took the first watch, followed by Terry and finally El Capitano, who triumphantly took us into the Marina. This was to be 'Narooma's new home for the foreseeable future. To this end, there were several lockdown jobs to be completed before we left the following morning to catch our plane back to the U.K.

"Wrighty, I have another little job for you."

"Don't tell me. You want me to climb up the main mast and change the light bulb?"

"No! I wouldn't dream of asking you to do that, unless we were at sea!"

Tone said, with a smile creeping across his suntanned face.

"No, easy one. Get the dinghy, bucket and sponge and give the hull a quick wipe over to wash off the salt and sand we gathered on the trip down".

Actually, I enjoyed the job. The only problem was trying to wipe down the hull as instructed, standing in the dinghy!

I kept falling over into the marina every time I put pressure on the hull, as the dinghy pushed backwards. It was a hot day, and it was an excellent way to keep cool! My shipmates were busy making sure all things were battened down with ropes and the equipment was correctly stowed. We stopped mid-afternoon for late lunch, which was initially on the deck, but the heat made us beat a retreat back into the relative cool of the salon. After a spot of lunch, we went for a wander around the marina, admiring the colourful orchids which were in great abundance. Tone had to pop into the office to settle up and finalise a long-term mooring contract, as this was the nearest marina to Tony and Camilla's Spanish home near Henares, Andalusia, some forty to fifty miles north.

Our last evening was once again spent on the deck eating fine cuisine, washed down with copious amounts of local, ridiculously cheap wine. After this eventful voyage, we were all in a reflective mood, especially aided by the copious amounts of alcohol! Collectively, we still wondered if the taxi driver in Gibraltar was still struggling with the Barbary ape, to prevent more damage to his vehicle. My two shipmates declared the funniest thing for them was watching me change the pointy end light bulb!

We stayed on the deck until the sun went down, where we could see the other boats in the marina lit up, with their crews enjoying the experience.

"Well, shipmates, here's toast to us and 'Narooma'," said Tone, raising his glass.

"'To us and 'Narooma'" we all echoed.

I must confess, the following morning, to having a pang of regret, as we piled into the taxi to take us to Malaga airport for the flight back to the U.K., but what an experience, that would stay with me always.

10 U.S.A TO AFRICA TO AUSTRALIA

While me and my two shipmates had an adventure on the high seas, Hayley reprised her role as 'Anna' in the musical "The King and I", for which she had previously gained critical acclaim, touring Australia in the early nineties. However, this planned tour would take in many U.S. major cities over a year or so. In a letter, she expressed her excitement at the prospect of the tour. Hayley played the part for some twelve months before having to prematurely pull out, having slipped on the bathroom floor and breaking a toe against the door! However, Hayley was back in the States in 2000, performing in an aptly named "A Suite in Two Keys". The production consisted of two separate plays, the first being "Shadows of the Evening" followed by "A Song at Twilight". Hayley produced two impeccable roles, as a fading English rose in one play and a quiet, but strong German character in the other, for which she won an award. In a letter to me, Hayley expressed her thought that although the roles and production were challenging, it was an interesting experience, and she would have not missed it for the world!

My mother always had an expression, “as one door closes, another opens”, and this was surely the case for Hayley in the following year, when she said farewell to her lovely old home in Hampton and moved into London. I am totally in agreement when Hayley said she was sad to shut the door on the old house, but change is good, inevitable and exciting! I felt exactly the same when we left ‘Skeete Place’, our lovely old farmhouse in Kent, and moved North! It must be confessed, both Joe and myself have fond memories of Hayley’s home in Hampton, especially the music hall mirror ensconced in a wing of the house. Apparently, it was a work of art to get it through the door in one piece! I adored her hallway with the black and white tiles, plus the impressive staircase with masses of photographs of famous faces adorning the wall. For me, what made it homely was the bicycle propped up in the hall alongside muddy football and boots!

Hayley, on one occasion, had invited me to one of her birthday parties at this home, but I had arrived far too early. After knocking the front door a couple of times, it suddenly opened with Hayley in a dressing gown, trying desperately to pile her wet hair up on top of her head and secure it with a towel!

The rear walled garden, which was an absolute delight to enter, felt like stepping back in time with its swing and orchard, and I always thought what a great place for her boys to grow up in, and charge about with their freedom.

Hayley also had an apartment in New York, which served her well, considering the amount of work coming from the States. However, 2004 saw Hayley back in her new London home, performing in a play called “The Perfect Games”, at the King's Head in Islington. Not often will you find a pub with a complete theatre upstairs! A really cosy pub with a fire burning merrily in the hearth, which always adds to the atmosphere, especially on a cold winter's day.

The following year 2005 was an incredibly heartbreaking year for Hayley and her siblings, Juliet and Jonathan. Sadly, their dad, Sir John Mills, passed away peacefully at his Denham home, on the 23rd April, at the age of ninety seven, and laid to rest at the church of St. Mary the Virgin in Denham village. To compound the family's grief, their mother, Lady Mills, also passed away the same year on 1st December. They had spent sixty four years together. What lives so well spent too. Churchill said once we might cause a ripple on the water during our lives, but once we are gone, the water goes flat and calm again. There are always exceptions to every general rule, and I believe the Mills family fits the criteria. In some way, their ripple will remain forever in the history of film, books, theatre and television! I was lucky enough to meet Sir John twice at Hayley's Hampton home. The first time was a fleeting call, but the second time was on Hayley's birthday, where I was invited for a cuppa, and a slice of cake! He was regaling us with amusing anecdotes from the theatre. My favourite, which actually he wrote into his autobiography, was once when he was playing the part of an English officer, who was mortally wounded in the first world war. He has to do a dying act, which, he said with a twinkle in his eye, is the dramatic moment every actor worth his salt enjoys! Having delivered his lines with great anguish, he said he laid prostrate centre stage, keeping as still as humanly possible. Then, a German officer walks over and bends over Sir John to ensure he has expired. When suddenly without warning, the first world war helmet, complete with its spike, drops from the German officer's head and unfortunately speared Sir John in a delicate part of his anatomy! Our hero wasn't sure who was the most startled! He suddenly came back to life, with the

German officer equally leaping back in total shock! Using his skills at improvisation, he immediately died again in more pain - literally!

When I had the craft shop and tearooms in Alston, one of the items we used to trade in was vinyl records, mostly second hand, but every now and again, a totally unused record would emerge that had been stored in a person's attic forever! The one in this instance was a vinyl collection of Noel Coward's songs, still in it's sealed packaging! Hayley had mentioned her dad was a keen collector of vinyl, and knowing the personal connection between Noel Coward and her family, it seemed fitting to forward this on to her dad. It was Noel Coward who watched John Mills when he performed for a repertory company called the 'Quaints', out in Singapore during the thirties. The play, entitled "Mr Cinders", had the leading man, John Mills, making an entrance on roller skates, carrying a clutch of parcels. The upshot was as he careered around the uneven stage at great speed. Unfortunately, one skate got caught and launched him spectacularly, before crashing onto the stage! The audience thought it was part of the show, and howled with laughter, whereas John wanted to howl with pain, especially as he had dislocated a finger! After this entrance, John Mills could do no wrong with the audience, who were laughing at every comedic line. Afterwards, Noel Coward went backstage and congratulated John on a super show, especially the entrance. When informed it was an accident, Noel Coward's amused comment was:

"My dear boy, an entrance such as that is pure gold, you must keep it in."

As I previously mentioned, "Ice Cold in Alex" was my favourite John Mills film, out of the one hundred and twenty films he appeared in! For his contribution to the film industry, the Queen knighted him in 1976.

In fact, his career spanned seven decades. He was the consummate actor. John Mills had the courage and vision of his convictions and a belief in his talent, which gave him that determination to succeed. He had come from a modest background, with his first job being a clerk, and later as a travelling salesman, selling toilet rolls, door to door! His first taste of the stage came at the tender age of six, in a school production.

His amazing zest for life, and especially for the stage. Even in his later years, he was still doing a one-man show, despite failing health and eyesight. He and Mary were married during the war, in 1941. Although he had enlisted for the army, he was later discharged on medical grounds. He then made several memorable films depicting the courage of the forces during the war conflict. Among them were "In Which We Serve", "We Dive at Dawn" and post war "The Colditz Story", "Above Us the Waves", "Dunkirk" and of course "Ice Cold in Alex", to name a few! He was awarded the BAFTA lifetime award for his work in the industry, in 2002.

Mary Hayley Bell was born on the other side of the world in Shanghai, China, but like John Mills, she also had dreams of the stage, making her debut with a touring American troupe in "The Barretts of Wimpole Street", in 1932. Her first appearance on the London stage was in 1934, in the play "Vintage Wine". Several other plays followed, with tours to New York and Australia. Mary put her acting career on hold when she met and married John, after meeting at the Comedy Theatre in 1939, and, of course, when the children came into their lives through the forties. Juliet made her debut entrance in 1941, with Hayley entering the stage in 1946 and Jonathan following up in 1949. Apart from writing her well known novel, "Whistle Down The Wind", in 1959, and co-writing a few years later, "Sky West and Crooked",

Mary had also written dialogue for "Scot of the Antarctic". She also penned four plays, "Men in Shadow", "Duet for Two Hands", "Angel" and "The Uninvited Guest", through the forties and early fifties. " Whistle Down the Wind" was certainly my favourite, both as a novel, film and later in 1996, as Andrew Lloyd Webber's musical adaptation for the stage.

Much of their married life was shared with charging around the planet on theatre tours, or making films on locations, but they enjoyed a strong bond as a family. Home was either the farm in Cowden, on the borders of Kent and Sussex, or a few years later their beautiful Georgian home, 'The Wick', on Richmond Hill, which incidentally, they purchased on two separate occasions! After the first sale, they desperately missed The Wick, and by chance they actually managed to repurchase it when it became available after a few years. Hayley wrote a charming letter to me in June 2009, saying Juliet, Jonathan and her were all together in London, and they had decided to visit their old beloved home on Richmond Hill, and take a photograph.

Later, Sir John and Lady Mary would spend their twilight years in the splendid "Hills House" in Denham, a property the young John Mills often admired as he passed on his way to nearby film studios. As health issues continued to increase, they moved to a more manageable bungalow in Denham, where they spent the remainder of their days.

It is difficult to imagine the intense pain Hayley and her two siblings felt losing both parents within such a short time, but what two great, and well spent lives to celebrate!

A few years later, in 2013, my father, or Pop as I called him, also sadly passed away. Similar to Sir John, Pop had lived to the great age of ninety seven, being born in 1915 in Folkestone, Kent. He, like many others, experienced the harsh realities of post First World War Britain, especially during the twenties. Money was especially tight for the

Wright family after his dad lost his job as a customs officer at the nearby harbour. Even though still at school, Pop had three jobs to help put bread on the table. Of course, there was no welfare system in place, so it was the case of all hands on deck! Although tough times, Pop said it was always a happy home, with lots of laughter. He was a popular local character, with one of his party tricks being to swim around the Folkestone harbour, no mean feat! Probably, I suspect to impress the local young ladies! Mother was a little wary when she first met him, as she knew of his reputation, which preceded him. After their first date, he foolishly bragged to his friends he had knocked up another conquest, totally without any justification. The result was when his mother heard the rumour, she was absolutely livid, and promptly blew him out of the door! It took a massive amount of grovelling to regain her respect! They married in September 1938, just prior to the second world war. My eldest sister, Carol, or little big sister, as I affectionately call her, arrived on the planet in 1939. Sister number two, Julia, arrived in 1940, with me tailing behind in March 1945.

Pop was shipped off to the North African campaigns in 1942, with further action in Italy, arriving finally in southern Germany in early 1945. He said many German villages and towns welcomed them as welcoming victors and cheered them on. On one such occasion, a young girl ran out into the road in her excitement, and Pop took the view that she might get hurt with the heavy military traffic passing through. So using his initiative, he broke rank and ran over to the youngster, scooped her up and placed her back on the pavement. For his efforts to save the young 'fraulein', Pop was placed on a charge of fraternising with the enemy!!!! Technically, the army was correct, as it was February 1945, and war did not cease until 7th May 1945. However, no penalty was ever awarded in the circumstances.

Of course, the dates betray the fact that Pop could not be my biological father. He had gone to war having two little daughters, and came home to two daughters and a cuckoo in the nest! Mother was only twenty five when she gave birth to me. She had not seen her husband for a few years. She had experienced hellish German bombing raids, especially as Folkestone was a frontline target, alongside nearby Dover. Both being active military ports. Imagine the terror when the doodlebugs and the V2 Rockets started their relentless attack. On one such attack in 1941, my mother decided to walk the short distance to her father's home, with my two sisters, at Mead Road House in Folkestone. Apparently, he was sunbathing in his back garden. After a bit of deliberation, he finally made up his mind and went with them up to the town centre shops. Just as they finished shopping, the warning siren went and they all dashed to the nearest underground shelter! For what seemed forever, they sat huddled in the semi gloom as the lights kept flickering whilst the enemy dropped their lethal cargo! After the siren signalled the all clear, they emerged back into the daylight, and made their way home. On arrival, they found Mead Road had been cordoned off. Mead Road House had been totally destroyed with a direct hit! The shopping trip had saved my grandad's life! On top of these horrors, she was bringing up two little girls, and having to take in military lodgers if a spare room was available. My biological father was one such lodger, except the lodger became more than just the lodger! Apparently he was an American pilot and, as such, might have got caught up with the 'D Day' landing in June 1944, something I will never know. My conception would have been early June 1944, as I arrived on the planet early in March the following year. Pop, when he returned from war, near the end of April or the beginning of May 1945, must have been in a state of deep shock. When he was posted abroad in 1942, he had a wife and two small daughters. On his return, he had a wife, two young daughters, and an extra mouth to feed! After exploring some heated options, one of them being to put the little cuckoo into an orphanage, Pop marched up to town, registered me as his, and whilst near the shops, he bought a bunch of roses and some chocolate for his young wife. A simple token of their mutual love despite everything. Mother was just twenty six years old and pop thirty. It is a testament to that generation how they managed to overcome the ravages of war, and survive to settle down to a post war Britain.

It was not until being a nine year old lad that the truth came out. I was playing with some toys, when an Aunt, my mum's sister, who, up until that moment, was a favourite, suddenly burst into the room and shrieked at me:

"You know your bloody dad is not your actual dad! You're nothing but a bloody bastard!" I just stared in disbelief as more verbal garbage came my way. Disbelief turned into tears, and I ran from the room. Apparently, my aunt had fallen out with her sister, and wanted to score points, with me becoming the target! Fortunately, I ran into the arms of my eldest sister, who would have been about fifteen at the time. She explained yes, it was true, but it would have to stay a secret, as it would cause even more family problems. I couldn't talk to my mother, or anyone for that matter, just had to keep it to myself. Imagine how it felt staring across the dinner table later that day looking at your dad, knowing in fact, he wasn't your biological father! I just had to adjust to this knowledge and deal with it, to the best of my ability! My mother, on odd occasions, wondered why I didn't visit my Aunt as much, but I managed to evade the genuine answer.

The subject never came up for discussion, except just before mother's death in 1995. I visited her at her home in

Kent, and she suddenly said she needed to tell me how she had been a wicked, wicked young woman many years ago, towards the end of the war! Immediately, it struck a chord, insomuch it made me aware how she had shouldered the guilt for all these decades. The fact that her husband, on returning from war, had actually forgiven the infidelity, probably compounded her own guilt! We both shared the way society dealt with such issues at that time. It was all swept under the carpet, and no word was spoken about it! My reaction to my mother's possible confession was simple:

"Gosh, mother, you told me all about that years ago!"

"I did?"

"Yes, that's all water under the bridge!" A smile crossed her face as she followed up with:

"I'm a silly old woman, aren't I? I forget so much these days!" which was perfectly understandable, as she suffered from Alzheimer's disease!

Interestingly, I took Pop out for a meal the same evening. With the conversation with my mother still foremost in my mind, I felt it would be an expedient time to bring up the issue with him.

"Hey Pop, I just want to say a big thank you to you."

"Don't thank me, you're paying!"

"No, not the meal! But the situation concerning my birth. I have known since I was nine years old! And of course, the dates didn't make sense. Of course, I give thanks to my biological parent, otherwise I wouldn't be here now, but you were my father and always have been".

I reached across the table and placed a reassuring hand on him. His reaction personified his hurt of that time so long ago. He quickly withdrew his hand and quietly said:

"If your mother chooses to talk about it, that's her decision, but I am certainly not going to talk about it whatsoever!"

These two conversations were the only time in my life the question of my biological father was ever mentioned! It occurred to me that the three of us shared this secret, causing guilt, hurt and confusion! As a footnote, after Pop passed away in 2013, I had used a DNA kit, which proved positively my American heritage! However, Pop was always my dad, and always will be remembered as such.

After Mother died in 1995, Pop lived alone for a year, before my 'little, big, sister' came to his rescue. Evidently, he was not coping well. She and her husband scooped Pop up, and took him back to their Welwyn Garden City home, where he stayed until his death in 2013. He had led an active life, with only ever having three days off for sickness during all his working days, including the war years! On his last day, he still completed three walks around his locality, stopping and chatting to all and sundry. On arriving home, he retired to his own sitting room to watch the telly before going down to have tea with my sister and brother-in-law. My sister had popped up to his room to see what he would like for tea. He had replied he felt a little tired, but please return in a few minutes, and he would let her know. When she returned ten minutes later, he had quietly slipped away from this mortal world, to rejoin the great love of his life! It was a fitting tribute for my sister and brother-in-law, to fetch Pop's favourite whisky and raise a glass to our father in his comfy armchair!

Hayley wrote the most moving and eloquent testament to losing a loved one, especially a parent, when she wrote a condolence letter to me shortly after his death.

Dear Trevor,

I was so sorry to hear your father passed away. My sympathies and thoughts are with you and your family at this time. He was a wonderful age, a year older than my Dad, and because of that I thought he would live forever! Maybe somewhere inside you felt that having weathered so many of life's storms, he would just keep going. But how wonderful for him and for all of you that he died so quickly and peacefully. Just like my Dad. It's a great gift to those left behind. But the void will always be there, the world that was him, and you and all that life and those memories - are now just that, just memories. And gratitude. Memories, gratitude, and love.

Thinking of you,
With Love, Hayley x

This letter from Hayley is a most treasured example of her caring nature, by virtue of the sentiment displayed in her writing, and was greatly welcomed as a source of comfort.

11 FOUR LEGGED FRIENDS

What Issy Did Next

It would be impossible to complete this story without reference to my greatest equine friend, Issi, or Issipoo, as he was more affectionately known at the stables where he was kept. His original racing name was 'Azurelordpleases', which was a mouthful! His last race was at Uttoxeter in 1993, where his jump racing career came to an inglorious end. He went around the track for a few furlongs, in his normal last position, and then, without any warning, decided enough was enough! With the poor jockey holding on with grim determination, Issi swerved left, cleared the rail, and having scattered a few spectators thundered up the hillside into a small copse at the summit and out of sight! Bless his heart, he had never won anything during his career, or even placed!

Issi came into my life in 2001 after seeing an advert in a Newcastle-upon-Tyne newspaper. The first time I saw him at a stable in the Washington area, I immediately fell in love! Issi was a 16.3 hand bay thoroughbred gelding, and just shy of 17 hands after the farrier fitted new shoes! He had a distinctive, but delicate crescent shaped, white blaze on his forehead. The fact that he was being used for learner riders at a riding school spoke volumes about his laid back temperament. He adored attention, and like many horses, had an extra special tickle area! His was just behind the front legs on the tummy. His tongue would drop out one side of his mouth, while he would screw his head into the air. To complete the picture, Issi would often take one front hoof off the ground and wave it around! His favourite titbit was small molasses muffins, which were carefully monitored, otherwise he would have had steam coming out of his ears!

Occasionally, as a rare treat, he would enjoy the odd can of Guinness. I would remove the ring cap, and he would suck the can dry by tilting his head up. It amused me the way the can would gradually crumble under the grip of the suction! When finished, Issi would have this giant white foam smile!

His new home was a stable at Middle Bayles, just outside of Alston, on the road to Penrith. A large and airy stable block with several other horses to chat with. Apart from the full size, floodlit all weather arena and a training pen, there was this magnificent one mile track, which encircled several fields following winding paths and hidden valleys. My day would start with the routine of being at the stable at 8am every day, come rain shine. Issi would always have his head over the door waiting for me to arrive, especially as I was the bringer of his breakfast! After a suitable time to allow his food to digest, it would be time to groom. One of the tricks I taught him was when I tapped a leg to clean his hoof, and he would oblige by lifting accordingly. Naturally, it cost me a molasses muffin or two!

Riding in the spring could be a problem, as he had issues with the bunches of daffodils irregularly growing around the fields. Clearly to him, they were dangerous yellow dragons swaying in the breeze, waiting to attack and devour him! Inevitably, we would dance sideways past each bunch. I used to call it 'daffodil dressage'! Oddly, he had a similar problem with the sheep fraternity, especially if one came too close. Considering the northern fells are mainly used for sheep farming, we also developed the skill of 'sheep dressage'too!

The lady who ran the stables agreed he had no fire in his belly to make a racehorse. He was just a gentle laid back horse, with the exception of his daffodil and sheep issues!

With this in mind, I still had a swift wake-up call when I took Issi to explore the arena for the first time. We idly shuffled our way around the arena in his normal laid back fashion, leaving two distinct trenches in the sand behind us, where you would in ordinary circumstances leave a series of hoof prints! That is, until we turned to face a jump on the opposite side of the arena. Suddenly out of nowhere, something in Issi's memory box stirred. Perhaps a distant memory of the race track, which suddenly elevated his equine brain into total overdrive - I could not hold him! He was gone! We went full pelt towards the jump. It all became a blur. Suddenly, I felt the gut-wrenching acceleration as we launched into space, like a rocket at takeoff! This was followed briefly by flying through the air like a trapeze artist, and then the harsh reality of the undignified crash landing which followed. I had lost my stirrups on takeoff. It occurred to me in my scrambled mind, Issi and I were about to part company, especially as we approached the end of the arena at fifty zillion miles per hour, but somehow we both managed to turn the corner together. Extraordinarily, he then switched back into his laid back shuffle with his head down, and returned to his sleep mode!

I glanced over to where a few people had gathered to watch the riding fiasco. They had descended into uncontrollable hysterical laughter! One of them managed, eventually to remark Issi had taken off over the jump with some two feet of clearance, which was staggering in itself, but more intriguing, he had launched some eight feet from the jump!

On another occasion, I was riding out with a friend, Claudia, and her beautiful thoroughbred horse named Jim. When we arrived back at the stable, Claudia suggested we try the three jumps set up in the field adjacent to the arena. The three jumps were in a dead straight line. Claudia went first and demonstrated immediately she was a far more competent rider than myself. The perfect combination of horse and rider. Pure poetry in motion, whereas I tended to ride like a sack of potatoes balanced precariously on Issi's back! Now it was my turn. I trotted Issi down the field with an air of superficial confidence, and turned towards the line of jumps. Immediately, I was catapulted forwards at an incredible rate of acceleration. Claudia and Jim watched about half-way down the course. When she regained her composure from the hysterical laughter and dried her tears, her recollection of the event was as follows:

The thunder of hooves, "Oh fuck!", more thunder of hooves, "Oh fuck!" and even more thunder of hooves, "Oh fuck me!". The miracle was, I actually stayed on!

Although the stable had its own track, it was a pleasure to ride out onto the high fells, on a path directly behind the stable complex. The route took you to a trig point on the summit. From this scenic advantage, the views were stunning in all directions, with the dominant feature being the lofty summit of Cross Fell, the highest point of the North Pennines. Below, nestling in the valley, was Alston with its quaint houses and cottages, many of which date back to the early 1600's. The summer sunsets were magnificent from the summit. I always found peace here with time to reflect on life and the various paths you tread. whereas Issi in contrast was thinking "what on earth has possessed this human to expect me to haul him all the way up here, sit for a few moments, and then walk all the way back down again! And they are meant to be on top of the evolutionary tree! He had better give me a muffin or two when we get back!"

One of Issi's favourite games was conducted in the arena. He would be running free with no saddle or bridle. I would charge towards him, waving my arms about, yelling 'I'm coming to get you'. He would do that doggy stance of lowering his front and sticking his rear up. Just at the crucial moment when I tried to block his move, he suddenly flew past me at full gallop with his tail straight up! He would then wait for me at the other end of the arena to repeat the game. Sometimes he would get so excited, he would career down the arena doing incredible high bucks with his head between his front legs. It was a magnificent sight to witness. There was a lot of snorting and heavy breathing, but that was me! In the end, I would quietly walk up to him, and he knew instinctively, this signalled the end of the game. with a muffin coming his way.

The whole time I had Issi was a blessing. It was a great joy to ride and have a natter with the other people at the yard. I still miss that equine aroma and the sweet smell of hay, especially when first arriving at the stable each morning. Amazingly, I would also be greeted by a host of twenty-two jackdaws, patiently waiting close to the feed store. I would take a few handfuls of Issi's horse feed, walk round the corner, and sprinkle it on top of a low wall. Sometimes with their excitement, they would stand on my head or shoulders! There was one magical morning, where after feeding Issi in his box, I felt sleepy and sat out in the morning sun and dozed off. On coming to, there were twenty two jackdaws, also fast asleep around me, with many having their heads tucked under their wings. One of those rare moments in life never forgotten!

What Sam Did Next

Sam was my big German Shepherd companion, who in my transport days was my constant shadow. Everywhere I went, he went. Tipping the scales at just shy of eight stone, he was like Newhouse Edwin Elliot, the Aberdeen Angus bull on Rudy Sterberg's farm in Kent. Due to his weight, Sam could sometimes overwhelm you with his enthusiastic devotion! He would often stand on his hinds and place his front paws on your shoulders to ensure he had your total attention. Heaven help you if you toppled backwards, he would be straight on top and lick you to death! Apparently he was not a good specimen for a German Shepherd. He did not have the sloping back posture that many breeds possess, his was straight. This actually meant his hind legs were longer. The other feature which made him more cuddly was that he was a long coat version of the German Shepherd dog. A general thick mass of black and tan hair, which made him appear much larger than he was. The truth would be out, if he jumped into the sea or a river - his huge foxy looking tail would suddenly be transformed into a thin apology for a tail! For all his height and weight, he was a big softy, who loved everyone. Absolutely useless as a guard dog! This was borne out by a time when a new transport client unexpectedly came to our old farmhouse in Kent. The chap had come to our back door, but had no response, as we were both out. He glanced through the window into our living room and noticed Sam curdled asleep in the middle of the room. Perhaps it was the man's shadow as Sam arose from slumbers, padded over to the window, furiously wagged his tail as a greeting, before returning to his comfort zone in the middle of the room and curling up again, to return to his slumbers!

One of Sam's favourite pastimes was to play in the paddock we had built for the horses. I would sit Sam in the middle of the paddock and command him not to move. I would roll a ball past him. He would swivel his head to track the ball, but not chase after it. When it came to rest, he would look back at me for the signal to chase the ball, collect it, and return to my left-hand side, having circled behind me. By way of command, I would say, "On your marks, get ready, (pause) and go!" Like a rocket, he would hare off after the ball, scoop it up at a zillion mph, race back, circle behind me, place the ball at my left foot and sit down waiting for the next command. All accompanied by a furious amount of tail wagging!

Another great game was a general rough and tumble adventure in the paddock. The moment Sam saw me donning a thick old anorak and gloves, he was there ready to go. We would face each other at a distance. He would be sitting and I would stand. On the count of three, I would yell, "go!". We would launch at each other with great speed. He would invariably knock me over on impact, and proceed to drag me by my arms, legs, or anything else, come to that matter to prevent me leaving the paddock enclosure! To stop the game, all I had to do was tap Sam on his shoulders, and he would immediately switch off the attack mode and plonk himself beside me, panting and of course still wagging his tail. All good fun, but the reasoning I had was that the game released any aggressive energy, allowing him to travel through life, loving everyone and wagging his tail!

We have all heard how birds migrate using their built-in radar system. It did make me wonder whether other animals have a similar capability. When I had the transport business, there was a regular monthly run to Edinburgh from Kent, which I enjoyed doing myself. Sam would accompany us for the four or five days we were away from home. Over time, I had worked out the best service stations to stop at overnight. We would park the lorry and set off for an hour or two traversing the northern fells of England or the southern fells of Scotland, depending on where we stopped. Afterwards, Sam would tuck into his evening meal before retiring to the cab, and I would drift over to the transport part of the service area for food and a natter with other drivers. Generally speaking, the Edinburgh run was approximately one thousand miles as a round trip. Sam would spend much of his time asleep while I drove, but it never failed to astonish me that after all that distance and time, he would wake up instantly, the moment I took a left hand turning in the little village of Sellinge, just some four miles from home! He would sit bolt upright, staring intently, straight ahead, for the last leg of the journey. Perhaps animals, like birds, have a natural built-in radar system. Maybe we do too, but we lost the ability to naturally navigate, so we designed satnav!

When we first moved to Cumbria from Kent, we discovered the beautiful Talkin Tarn, located two miles from the country town of Brampton. Every morning, having seen Joe off to his primary school, his mum and me, plus our three dogs, Sam. Jack, and Kirsty, the latter two being Border Collies, would walk around the tarn following the scenic path through the woods to explore the small island linked by a narrow wooden bridge.

The surrounding land is farmed with boundary dry stone walls which run into the tarn. To gain path access, a gap of about a foot is left in the wall fabric. Enough to keep sheep in, but allow a person through. Sam had picked up a lengthy tree branch, which he was determined to hang onto at all costs. Unfortunately, no matter how he tried, he found it would not go through the wall gap! We stood and watched as Sam went backwards and forwards, headbutting the gap in the wall with no result, other than a sore mouth. Then he had a doggy eureka moment! He tracked the wall into the tarn carrying his treasured piece of tree, and when reaching sufficiently deep water, he swam over the wall and triumphantly walked back to the gap where we had just dodged through to watch him! There was much wagging of tail, and showering us with water, but he looked so pleased with himself

What Sabre-Thom Did Next

The first time I met Sabre Thomas was while visiting the Wetheral animal sanctuary in Cumbria with my son Joe during the summer of 1992. We had gone there with no intention of getting any pets, let alone a cat, as we already had Smudge at home. However, the upshot of the visit was that Sabre Thomas actually chose us! After having a refreshments in the sanctuary cafe, we wandered down to see the various animals. Eventually, we came to the cat enclosure, and while looking at the various feline residents, suddenly without warning, this jet black cat with an incredibly loud voice shot up the security fencing, until he was at eye level with us, and continued to explain with great indignation why he should not be there at all. It was abundantly clear to us, it would be necessary to go straight to the office and arrange his immediate removal to our home! We both fell in love with him and therefore complied with his wishes to obtain his release! Obviously, it was not as straightforward as Sabre had imagined. There was the question of checks to ensure we were suitable servants for Sabre Thomas, where his every feline whim could be catered for, and of course with the necessary funds to support his lavish lifestyle! The office staff at the sanctuary explained Sabre Thomas had been "arrested" for vagrancy in Carlisle alongside his brother, who had already been chosen by a member of the kennel team.

We were told we could pick Sabre up in two days. After leaving the office, we walked back to the cat enclosure to celebrate the good news. The moment we approached the cattery, Sabre Thomas shot up the fencing yelling, either because he loved us or hated us, depending whether we were taking him home with us there and then. I gently told him he would have to be patient for a few days. He wasn't particularly impressed, but I promised we would be back!

Both Joe and me were glad Sabre Thomas had selected us. He was such a character who brought a new dimension to our lives. His breed could loosely be described as 99% Siamese, but with the exception he was black and not the normal seal with brown points. He was of slim build, with pointy nose and lengthy tail. His eyes were green and his ears seemed to dominate his head, but the overriding factor was his incredible speaking voice! Although Sabre Tom was not particularly large as cats go, it was his charismatic personality which dominated the home. His first stage was to demote Smudge to second-in-command and to employ me and Joe as servants. From the get go, Sabre Thomas made us aware of the cuisine he expected, which cheered Smudge up no end, as his diet greatly improved too! Only the best would do!

Sabre's new home was our Back Garth home in Alston, which was an extraordinary building. The front elevation, viewed from cobbled through road, was dated 1732. The far end of the property had been a shepherd's cottage with a barn below to house his sheep built in 1611. Possibly an early form of central heating! The two buildings had become linked with a third construction in the Victorian era. From an aerial perspective, the whole building was 'L' shaped. Hayley said on one occasion, she was sure it must have a ghost, but added reassuringly, it would be of a friendly disposition! Being built into a bank, the front had three levels, with the craftshop and teashop on the ground floor. The second floor housed the bedrooms, bathroom and kitchen, and the third floor was the drawing room and dining room. Joe had the whole 1611 building. I made him a bedroom in the roof and stair well to reach it. Below was his playroom, where we installed a bar billiard table, to have him play before going to school in the morning.

I mention the shape of the house again for a pertinent reason. On one occasion, having locked the shop door for the day, Joe, the two cats, two dogs and I were relaxing on the third floor. Sabre Tom suddenly went into one of his mad, hissy fits, where he would charge around the room, leap over furniture including us, run up the curtains, knock things over, especially if they got in the way! Normally, he would naturally run out of steam and finally stop, to have a wash and a nap. However, on this occasion, he went too far. Literally! Having careered around the room several times, he launched himself to the open transom window and cleared it with ease! It was like a cartoon comedy sketch. With his velocity, he flew level for a couple of seconds until gravity took over, and he nose-dived from the three-storey building to the cobbled road below! Needless to say, we charged downstairs to the shop door, which we opened with great trepidation, expecting to see a squished black cat in the road. But no, in Sabre Tom walked with his tail bolt upright and said in his iconic loud voice "Prrrt, Prrrt!" Took him to the vets, who declared nothing broken, save only his spirit was left a little dented, having lost one of his nine lives!

The kitchen in the middle part of Back Garth had a stable door with stone steps, which led down, to an attractive courtyard, where on sunny days we would serve afternoon teas and cakes. On turning right from the stable door, you would find yourself in our secluded garden, which was home to various trees and a divine clematis. This huge botanical delight spread over the entire gable end of the adjacent bungalow. Every year, we would be treated to a massive display of spectacular buds. With a doubt, a cornucopia of colour!

I was clearing up the tea things in the kitchen one evening, when I heard the dreadful bloodcurdling cry of Sabre Thomas, who was sitting on the bungalow roof, squaring up to another cat. Sabre Tom was on the warpath at the sheer audacity of this intruder, daring to even think of entering his domain. Without warning, they attacked each other, both balancing on their hinds, using their front legs and paws to grip their opponent. Needless to say, they toppled over, but continued the fight as they rolled down the roof. There was a moment or two of silence as they rolled off the roof, before commencing the battle again! It did not phase either of them, the fact they had just rolled down and off a roof. The fight was a matter of principle! The final upshot being the intruder eventually decided, enough was enough, and sloped off into the gloom. On the other hand, Sabre Tom noticed me standing by the kitchen porch and ran over to greet me with a tail as usual in the upright mode. He explained in a loud voice how he had vanquished the enemy, and we could sleep easy in our beds that night!

Although we loved Sabre Tom to bits, he could be a tad trying at times, especially if he decided he was not getting the respect he deserved!

A classic example of this behaviour was evident on one occasion when I sat working at the kitchen table doing the shop accounts. As the paperwork was kept in one of the kitchen drawers, I would take the relevant paperwork and leave the rest in the open drawer. With my back to the drawer, I became acutely aware of running water. Naturally, I turned to see the source of this running water, only to find Sabre Thomas happily squatting on my paperwork in the drawer, bloody peeing! The moment I advanced on him, he had leapt over the stable door and gone! Incredibly, about thirty minutes later, he nonchalantly waltzed through the kitchen, tail bolt upright saying "prrrt, prrrt, prrrt" which loosely meant, well that was fun!

That was frustrating for me, but Joe also had issues with Sabre Tom's attitude. On several occasions, Joe and I would settle down to a game of bar billiards, only to be interrupted by a demented Sabre Tom, who would knowingly jump onto the table, scatter the balls in all directions, and disappear as quickly as he appeared. Poor old Joe would remonstrate with me the fact that he was usually winning, when Sabre Tom wrecked the game!

The tearoom was totally out of bounds to all the pets for obvious health and hygiene purposes, but Sabre Tom was a rule breaker by nature. The word 'No' was simply not on his radar! Bearing this in mind, we tried our best to ensure he remained outside, but he would outwit us by hovering by the exit door and surreptitiously slip in as a customer left. You can imagine how I felt when serving two elderly women who came to our tearoom for an afternoon cream tea. Having served their choice of tea plus scones complete with jam and cream, I turned to take another order from a nearby table. These two young tourists started to giggle and point to the table where the two elderly ladies were seated. I turned, and to my absolute horror, there was Sabre Tom on his hinds trying to reach up over the edge of the table and reach for the cream pot! Obviously, it was necessary to take prompt action. As I swiftly walked past the errant Sabre Tom, I unceremoniously scooped him up and moved towards the door to remove him. The sound of crashing china and the tinkle of cutlery hitting the floor abruptly stopped my exit. Sabre Tom was not giving up without a fight over the cream, as he was still firmly attached to the tablecloth! Fortunately, the two ladies were drinking their tea and not hurt at all. In fact, they were generous over the whole debacle and admitted they adored cats, and assured me they would be dining out on this story for somewhile! Needless to say, I replaced their meal free of charge, it was the least I could do. As for Sabre Thomas, although I put him outside, he was still determined to hang onto the tablecloth, as he could smell the spilt cream!

12 AFRICA REVISITED

After various projects in the U.S.A in the early 2000's, Hayley was offered the part of Caroline Du Pressis in the television series "Wild at Heart", which kept her busy from 2007 to 2012, appearing in thirty-nine episodes. Ashley Pharoah created the series and co-starred Stephen Tompkinson, Amanda Holden, Dawn Steele, and Lucy-Jo Hudson. The story follows the life of a vet who, with his family, moves from Bristol and sets up a veterinary practice on a game reserve in South Africa.

This was a welcome return to the African continent for Hayley, since her huge success with "The Flame Trees of Thika", back in the early nineties. She kept in touch, saying how much she enjoyed the whole experience, especially working with the animals. In one of the earlier letters, Hayley recounted a time whilst taking snapshots of the African landscape. She was revolving on her feet, with her eye on the camera, and suddenly realised she was staring at the lower chest of a giraffe! She said she had never run so fast! She mentioned that although the cast and crew were a seriously friendly and professional group, and a joy to work with, it was still always good to get back home for some 'me' time and catch up with Crispian to share his success with "Kula Shaker", and Jason, who at the time was involved in directing a new play at the New End Theatre in Hampstead. In the meantime, Firdous was busy, with Simon McBosney's Theatre de Complicite, performing in a play called "The Disappearing Number", which initially opened at the Barbican, before embarking on a European tour.

As well as working in South Africa, Hayley performed in the U.S.A. and also juggled time at home in London, enjoying the other man in her life, young Keshava, Crispian's son. Crispian and his wife had a second son called Hari. Jason and his wife also had two children, Solomon in 2016, followed by Evalina in 2017. My son, Joe and Debbie, produced two grandchildren, Jessica, who has now become a teenager, and Jasper, who enjoys being Jasper. Both Hayley and I absolutely adore our respective grandchildren, with the joy and pleasure of watching them develop into rounded human beings. The ideals so eloquently echoed by a quote from Hayley in 2010, which articulates so well the essence of her humanity:

"So, here's to a new decade, presided over by a 'blue moon'. And hope springs eternally that collectively and individually, we can make more of the right decisions than the wrong ones, and show our fellows more love and compassion, than fear and suspicion".

During 2012, Hayley was offered the part of 'Ursula' in the play, "Ladies in Lavender", based on the original book entitled "Lace in Lavender", written by William Locke in 1916. Charles Dance wrote a powerful screenplay version of the story, which was filmed in 2004, starring Judy Dench and Maggie Smith. On watching the film production, it left a lasting impression on Shaun McKenna, the playwright, who was later invited to write a stage adaptation of the story.

Although in contact for years, I had not actually caught up with Hayley for a while, so I decided to treat myself and see the play when it was presented at the "Cambridge Arts Theatre" at Cambridge, in June 2012.

It is a long haul down to Cambridge from my home in Cumbria. Having said that, the first forty miles are incredibly beautiful, as the winding fell road twists its way across the North Pennines, before tumbling down the Tees valley to the historic town of Barnard Castle, and finally to Scotch Corner where the mighty A1M will take you virtually all the way to Cambridge non-stop! I arrived in the famous University city with enough time to park and walk to the theatre, which lies in the shadow of the university.

The play tells the story of two elderly women who discover a young man unconscious, apparently washed up on a nearby beach, and take him home and nurse him back to good health. Seemingly, dormant passions are ignited in the two women, with the added complication of a third, much younger woman arriving on the scene. For me, the production was beautifully constructed, conveying the poignancy of the two elderly women's friendship and the emotions uncovered as the play develops.

As always, as a matter of courtesy, I had contacted Hayley once the ticket was booked to say I would attend the production, and was it okay to bang on her door after the matinee show? I received a card back saying she would be most upset if I didn't! After the cast had their curtain call and disappeared, I trundled out into the bright June sunshine and wandered round to the stage door. Very kindly, Hayley had left a note with the doorman, indicating Trevor Wright would be calling by. One of his colleagues guided me through the labyrinth of theatre corridors to Hayley's dressing room. I banged on the door and a voice called out:

"Who is it?

"Trevor"

"One moment Trevor!"

After possibly two or three moments, the door opened, and a beaming Hayley greeted me with the added bonus that Firdous was there too. We talked for a while, and as always, Hayley asked after Joe, Debbie and Jessica, and naturally I wanted to hear her news relating to her grandchildren. Hayley was intrigued with the short film I had been in earlier, in April 2012, where I portrayed a very grumpy grandad, who had his very young granddaughter dumped on him for the weekend. They have a mutual dislike for each other! It was mainly located in and around Stoke-on-Trent. The twelve-year-old actress, Charlotte Dowson, was brilliant in her role. She actually reminded me of the young Hayley at that age. Masses of enthusiasm, the way she enjoyed the sets and the production crew, in fact her greatest prize was to be given the clapper board! Charlotte participated in the BBC series "Ordinary Lies", during 2015. For me personally, the hardest part of the film was having to carry the tired 'Jessica' up three flights of high-rise stairs, along a rather protracted corridor to my 'flat' door, fumble in my pocket for the door key, push the door open with my foot, progress through to my front room, and lower 'Jessica' onto a settee and cover her with a blanket. The cameraman was in front to start with, filming me coming up towards him. From that point, he would follow me. It took sixteen takes! The poor cameraman tripped over, going backwards up the stairs. I accidentally caught 'Jessica's' head on the wall on another take, and bless her, she did not complain at all! Another time, I had done the whole scene sequence, got to the settee and accidentally dropped her top part, and I was left holding her legs. The production team and Charlotte's mum howled with laughter, as did 'Jessica', with the director nervously looking at his watch! Charlotte, being just twelve, probably weighed about six stone, but after sixteen takes she felt like ten tons!

Firdous, tapping his watch, indicated Hayley had to go for a meal before the evening performance. I followed them to the stage door, where they were met with several people requesting autographs. I disappeared back to the carpark and down to my little-big-sister at Welwyn Garden City to spend the night. I had a good natter the following day, before setting off to the wilds of the north!

Hayley's professional life continued with a part in the popular, iconic "Midsomer Murders" television show in 2014, playing the part of 'Lizzy Thornfield' in the episode entitled "Wild Harvest". While Hayley worked on the "Midsummers" set, 2014 proved an eventful year for me too. I have played in groups since being thirteen years old, with one of my dreams being to set up a music festival. The local Alston ice cream man, a chap by the name of Ray Miller, or more affectionately known locally as 'Millie', and myself, had frequently talked about it over the previous year, with me propped against his ice cream van. Finally, in 2013, we decided to go for it! Armed with no experience or funding, we set to, and formed, a committee with similar interests, who could bring their individual talents on board. Our local Alston parish council allowed the festival use of the Tyne Willows Field. A beautiful site bordered by the famous River Tyne South, on the west side, and woodland encompassing the southern edge. These all, with the dramatic North Pennine fells, as a backdrop. Since it was the first outing in 2014, we proceeded with caution by making it a one-day event. It has now progressed to a two-day festival, with three stages. The Giddy Aunt Stage, which resembles a circus tent, the Over The Moon marquee, complete with stage, and green room for performers, but also leaving a large audience standing, or seating area. The third stage is attached to the Festival Bar, and called the Buskers Corner, where anyone can rock up and perform. The ethos of the festival is family orientated, so three or four children's entertainers wander the site to amaze the youngsters with their various artistic skills. We usually engage twenty, or so bands over the weekend, encompassing many genres of music, such as rock, blues, jazz, folk. It is great to see the field full of camping tents, and people enjoying themselves. Sadly, 2019 was the last Music Festival to be staged due to the pandemic, but we will be back!

The following year, a letter dropped into my postbox from Hayley explaining she was off to the other side of the planet to perform in a play called “Legends”, on a four-month tour of Australia. This was a brilliant opening for Hayley, as this comedic play written by ‘James Kirkwood’ concerned the lives of two ageing actresses, who detested each other, with the other character being none other than her own sister Juliet! It must have been fun, especially as they adore each other in the real world. It was certainly a family affair, as Juliet’s husband, Maxwell Caulfield, played the role of the optimistic producer, who desperately tried to raise money to produce a fictional play called “Craps”, and embarked on a money-making scheme to put on the Broadway production.

Back home, 2015 was proving to be an extremely stressful year. Sadly, just as Hayley was setting off on her Australian tour, I experienced one of those events in life which becomes etched on your mind for all time. The attached cottage next door, dating back to 1611, caught fire! It was about 3.30pm on the 17th April, when a panic struck. A local woman, who was delivering a prescription to my next-door neighbour, banged on my door, saying she had knocked next door and entered, but realised the place was already alight! I grabbed a towel, soaked it in water, threw it over my head, and entered my neighbour’s blazing home. The heat and smoke were intolerable. The dense black smoke extremely compromised visibility. Against this blackness, making a more horrific scene, was my neighbour, totally engulfed in flames. A silhouette in the midst of a flaming inferno. Without going into the true horror of the scene, it was clear he was deceased and nothing could be done to save him.

His cottage had a gas installation, whereas my property does not. In the circumstances, it seemed eminently sensible to vacate immediately and move the growing crowd back from our courtyard. The fire officers were contacted and were on the scene within ten minutes. The interior of the cottage was completely destroyed. Sadly, my neighbour, an ex-soldier who had served in both the Bosnian conflict and the Iraq war, had perished in the flames. Oddly, the cat who lived next door and survived the flames decided to adopt me! My cat,'Mr Paws', was a trifle sniffy at first, but grudgingly allowed this 'cuckoo' to share our home.

The same day, Tup North Productions were staging a one-off musical event for the community at the local town hall, featuring Sally Barker, who was a runner up in the television talent show "The Voice". As I was active in the production of the show, it was necessary to be there at the planned time of 6.30pm to meet with Miss Barker. The old maxim of 'the show must go on' rang true, and so it did. To give credit to Sally Barker, she put on an amazing professional concert. Certainly a consummate artist, who had toured with top headliners such as Tom Jones and Bob Dylan. From a personal perspective, the show detracted a little from the earlier horror of the fire.

After Hayley returned from Australia in the summer of 2015, she indulged in her favourite pastime of spending time with her grandchildren, before taking on the role of the Fairy Godmother in "Cinderella", in one of her favourite venues, "The Richmond Theatre", in south west London.

By chance, I had arranged to spend Christmas 2015 with Joe and his family, down near Folkestone. While down there, Joe and my daughter-in-law mentioned they might like to take the children to a pantomime, so I jumped in straight away with the suggestion we took them to Richmond, to see Hayley in "Cinderella". We booked the tickets, and I contacted Hayley to see if it was okay to meet backstage after the show. Her reply was yes, of course, especially as she had not seen Joe for some while and had never met the grandchildren.

Wednesday, 30th December 2015, saw the family in two cars driving up to Richmond, on a beautiful sunny but chilly day. I had the children, which was a huge treat. To cover the driving time, we counted how many red cars went past us, how many lamp posts per mile on the M25, and, of course, the obligatory, 'I spy', littered with:

"Grandad, are we nearly there?"

"Yes, nearly there", lying through my teeth as we passed a sign saying Richmond was another twenty miles! Eventually, we arrived at Richmond, and we were fortunate to find parking beside the park.

We joined the crowd at the entrance and eventually found our seats. I have always loved the atmosphere in the theatre prior to the curtain being raised, more so during the festive season, where everyone is in a great place, especially with so many children there to share the pantomime experience. The show was spectacular from start to finish. There were masses of one-line jokes delivered by the cast, especially Matthew Kelly, which kept the pantomime bouncing along. Hayley mentioned later, the pantomime was indeed fast and furious, and sometimes she wondered where she actually was in the show, to keep her entrance cues right, especially being the fairy godmother, so popping up frequently throughout the show! Pantomime can change on a nightly basis. For a start, the audience differs each time. There is usually a lot of ad-libbing between the cast and the audience. Children can really get caught up in the moment, with screaming at the top of their voice: “It's behind you”. Of course, the cast will rise to the comedic challenge and bounce back with one-off streams of banter!

Personally, I adore pantomime. To date, I have written and directed three. The first was “Jack and the Beanstalk',' with the first characters on the stage being Captain Hook and his motley crew. It has to be entertaining, but very much bonkers! I love to get pantomime characters crossing over! In that production, I wanted a beanstalk that would grow from a seed into a massive plant in front of the audience! This was a challenge for the set designing team, but they certainly came up trumps. As it grew, the plant even had big, coloured flowers which opened. To complete the illusion, behind the beanstalk was a ladder, where Jack could wave to the audience through portholes in the trunk, as he ascended the plant! The second Pantomime was “Cinderella the Sequel”. To make it different, I started the story from the end of the traditional yarn, where the Prince marries Cinderella and lives happily ever after in the castle. The obvious ploy was to cause a massive problem, with the alleged rumour, the Prince was having an affair with one of the ugly sisters! The upshot was, as the nasty Sheriff of Nottingham was involved, Cinderella and Buttons were unceremoniously thrown out of the castle. However, Robin Hood comes to the rescue, and all is explained, with Cinderella and the Prince reunited. All great fun! The third pantomime was “Aladdin”. Although, basically, we followed the traditional storyline, I took the gamble to include some real magic, which would involve random members of the audience. It was based on a mathematical trick, passed on by our maths teacher, while at school some sixty years ago! I had only ever tried the trick as a 'one on one' situation, and never with an audience. The essence of the illusion rested solely with the two characters who performed it. They had to be sure how the mechanics of the illusion worked. This was done in front of a closed curtain. What the audience was unaware of was me, pacing up and down the stage behind the curtain, chewing my nails to the quick, in case it went horribly wrong! Every performance worked perfectly, even to the extent we had the mind-read number already printed on a sheet of paper, under the first seat in the sixth row, by the central gangway. We knew the number before the audience arrived! Now that is magic! The theatre was situated in the upper level of our town hall. The producer and I thought it would be a great idea to have the cast lined up on the staircase, so the audience could have a quick banter as they descended to the exit. I would be the last person before they left. It was surprising how many people either asked me how the illusion was created or offered a solution, as they thought they knew how it worked! To the former, I said I am not allowed to disclose the solution, and to the latter, I simply urged them to keep their idea of a solution to themselves, even though no-one came close to the actual answer!!!!

Back in Richmond, after watching Hayley perform in the pantomime, we gradually joined the happy throng of excited young children, with their mums and dads, heading towards the exit. I turned to the two children and asked:

"How would you like to meet the fairy godmother?"

"What, for real Grandad?"

"Oh yes indeedy, Jessica."

"Oh wow! Yes please!" replied a very excited granddaughter.

"Can we have a go in the carriage grandad?"

"Mmmmm, not sure about that Jasper, my boy."

"Ohhhhhh," came the obligatory sound of disappointment!

We all trooped around the theatre block to the stage door, where it was, understandably, quite busy. I had a word with the attendant on duty, who confirmed we were expected. It is always surprising that actors are on cue for their stage entrance, considering the honeycomb of corridors! Personally, I would be terrified of entering a random door and finding myself on stage in front of a few thousand people!!!

One of the stage hands was asked to show the way to Hayley's dressing room. As always, she made us welcome and was so thrilled to meet Joe again. After a lot of chatter, especially to the grandchildren, where she found she had to explain why she was in jeans and jumper, as opposed to a fairy godmother dress, Hayley came up with the magic words:

"Who would like to walk onto the stage?"

"Oh yes please!" said the five of us in unison!

Through my friendship with Hayley over the years, it has been an enormous privilege to step out onto some well-known theatre stages. In my own right, I have played many, many venues in the south and north of England, but they were mainly village, civic and community halls, plus pubs and clubs! Theatres have this wonderful atmospheric ambience around them, where all the facets of stagecraft are delivered from high drama to comedy, from Shakespeare to pantomime. A world opposite to the norm. Actors already know the words they must speak, whereas we usually have to think before we open our mouths. Mind, having said that, sometimes we don't!!!

It was a picture looking at the grandchildrens' faces as they entered the stage and stared up at the seats where we had been sitting but a short while ago. This viewpoint of a traditional theatre is awesome, with the stalls sloping upwards away from the stage, and above them tiers of circle seats, rising high to the roof! There was quite a chorus of 'Oh wow', emanating from the two children.

"Who would like to see the carriage?" Hayley suddenly asked.

After several 'me's, had been shouted with great glee, we were taken into a wing of the stage where, hiding behind the flap, was the stagecoach. The ponies had already been unhitched and disappeared back to their local stables, which I was eternally grateful for. Otherwise, I had a vision of careering around the stage in a carriage at full gallop!

This was a fitting finale to our visit backstage, as always there is limited time available to the cast, before preparing for the evening show.

Hayley escorted us back to the stage door, where we said our farewells, and returned to our vehicles to drive back to Folkestone. The winter sunset soon gave way to inky blackness on the M25, giving me a chance to reflect on my life, especially as the children were travelling back with their mum and dad.

Looking back, Hayley, who had an extraordinary career in films, theatre, and television alongside her older sister Juliet, and younger brother Jonathan, was born into an incredibly talented family, with her much loved parents, Sir John Mills and Lady Mary Mills at the helm.

Apart from Sir John's natural acting talent, his determination and perseverance to succeed in the career he loved so dearly was helped by the chance meeting with Noel Coward in the thirties, who recognised his talent.

It was by the same twist of fate in 1963, I happened on probably the most famous teenager in the world. Yes, I will freely admit, like millions of others on the planet, I was enraptured by the quintessential English rose who was dominating the movie world. However, from that first meeting, after discovering fame is but an illusion, I found myself engaging with a kind and beautiful spirit. I was talking to Hayley Mills, the person, not Hayley Mills, the world-famous personality. In truth, at that point, I did not realise that our two lives, although totally different, would criss-cross over the decades with many, many letters and cards being exchanged. Indeed, an incredible story which needed to be told.

Looking back, I believe the pivotal reason this platonic relationship has endured is based on two free spirits acknowledging one another. As I have said, even at the age of four, I knew I was part of something magical. For me, the most magical part was to produce, alongside my wife at that point, another beautiful and kind spirit, in the form of my son Joe. Then the incredible magic of experiencing running with horses, a sea adventure, the years of music, writing, and so much more! To cap this, to meet Hayley by sheer chance back in 1963 and remaining friends to the current day. Absolute magic. The odd thing too, which I mentioned to her not so long ago, was that in all the years we have known each other, there is no single photograph of us! She said at the time, we would have to remedy this on my next visit south. Unfortunately, the pandemic swept across the planet, which obviously has curtailed any photographic opportunities! Strangely, although it would be great to have photographs, memories are far more powerful. For me, one such memory would be sipping wine, enjoying the late summer sunshine, seated next to Hayley on the garden swing, and having a chat at her Hampton home, with her two lads chasing around the garden

13 THE LAST WORD IS LEFT TO HAYLEY

It would be a fitting tribute that Hayley should leave the last words. After sifting through the collection of letters received from her over all these decades, I have cherry picked just a few suitable quotes from her correspondence to reflect Hayley's generosity of spirit, her kindness, and caring nature.

7th July 1975

"Whatever you do, wherever you are, I do with you."

1st November 1976

"Crisp started at school today, he found kindergarten very exciting. Your choice of Watership Down was great. I have read the paperback, but this will be something really beautiful for them both to read and enjoy, always."

27th April 1978

"The play is called Hush and Hide, it's a Victorian mystery, and we hope it will go to London - so keep your fingers crossed!"

17th August 1978

"It would give me great pleasure to offer you both coffee or something stronger, as you are going to be in London. If this sounds like a good idea, let me know which afternoon would be best, and I can give you directions. Once again, it's wonderful news - I'm very happy for both of you. Lots of luck."

10th May 1979

"We had a wonderful hot holiday, and we had the boys with us, and for a few weeks NOTHING to do except sunbathe! Now it is back to the grindstone."

23rd April 1980

"It was such a good birthday this year. I didn't mind getting older, which is quite extraordinary. I do hope you are both enjoying life to the full and feeling extremely well - that is so important, is it not!"

6th April 1981

"It is wonderful to be home again, at last we can concentrate on getting the house straight. Hanging curtains and pictures and getting cupboards built - we still have rooms full of packing cases, we look like a family of squatters!"

21st September 1981

"My heartfelt thanks for the beautiful flowers on the occasion of the first transmission of 'Flame Trees'. It was such a sweet thing to do. It was strangely nerve racking when the series came out, largely because I'd never seen any of them and had no idea how it would be received by the critics and the public. But I am happy to say, the reactions have been favourable. We even beat 'Crossroads' in the ratings!"

14th October 1981

(Having received news of my wife's pregnancy)

"I just had to write to say how delighted I am at your wonderful news. You both must be over the moon!"

19th April 1982

"Hampton is looking up too! I had a wonderful surprise. A birthday BBQ party had been arranged in the garden - sunshine all afternoon. It was a wonderful way to spend a birthday, surrounded by all the people you love... concentrate on the work in hand. A play at the Lyric called Talley's Folley, I start rehearsals next week."

4th June 1982

"Many, many congratulations on the birth of your baby boy - it is the most wonderful thing in the whole wide world. My thoughts are with you both. I know the joy that you are feeling, and I am so happy, for I am sure he is absolutely beautiful."

23rd March 1983

"I was told you were in front that night, and I expected you to come round afterwards. I am so sorry you couldn't make it."

29th March 1984

"It was so sweet of you, and thank you so much for the absolutely beautiful bunch of flowers you sent on the last night of 'Dial M for Murder'. It was a superb evening, and the flowers are still going strong, believe it or not!"

24th October 1984

"I am always so interested in reading your letters - you have a very philosophical attitude that I very much appreciate. I have recently found Karma in one's life, which can sometimes have a very good and positive effect and an opportunity to for re-appraisal of one's attributes and needs etc. I know how vital a more philosophical and spiritual concept of life is; we are all on a journey. Everything we think and say is important to the progress we make."

30th December 1985

"The sequel film to the Parent Trap is finally happening, and I am off to New York on the 2nd January, and then onto Florida for five weeks where it will be shot on location. I must say, I'm looking forward to a bit of warm weather!"

14th April 1986

"It would be a pleasure to see you on my birthday, all of you if you wish. About 11.30 - noon? See you then. Love Hayley."

28th October 1987

(After the UK Hurricane)

"I hope you are not too devastated by the hurricane. We lost a big tree which shattered the gate. Luckily, nothing damaged the house."

1st February 1988

"I have also been working with an American writer on two projects...it has been, an interesting, and educational, to be involved in the initial creative process of putting a project together."

2nd April 1989

"Filming up the road in Shepperton Studio, which is so convenient it's almost ridiculous! It is called, appropriately 'Back Home'. It must be so inspiring to have a poet such as yourself in the family:

'ere the morning dew,
Has dried on the mountain grass.
As I looked up in awe and splendour,
I slipped o'er on my arse!"[1]

16th April 1991

"Your life sounds really exciting up there on your mountain top, snow drifts, blizzards, and dramas. It does sound beautiful and quite well away from the rat race. I'm leaving for Australia on the 24th to do 'the King and I' for a few months."

2nd July 1991

(The day Joe's and my lives were destined to alter)

"Hope all well with you and the family. My best love to you all. As ever, Hayley x"

9th August 1991

(Hayley had contacted her personal secretary to relay this message to me)

"This is just to let you know that your distressing letter addressed to Hayley arrived, but unfortunately, she does not return from Australia until the end of the month. I know she

---

[1] I had this poetical cartoon in the window of my teashop in the North Pennines, where most people thought it was quite funny, until three elderly ladies reprimanded me for such vulgarity in a public place!

will be in touch on her return. She passes on her regards and love."

24th April 1992

"I had a quiet birthday, which ended with me having a game of football in the garden. I think I am going into my second childhood!"

19th June 1992

"You and Joe sound as though you are making a good life together, and your new home sounds most intriguing! I expect you must have a ghost, but I am sure it will be a friendly one! I'm sure you are a good and loving father for your son, and that will go a long way to compensate for him not having his mum around."

10th October 1992

"Dear Trevor, I'd love to see you after the show. Please do come backstage afterwards, Love Hayley x"

4th January 1993 (From New York)

"I do hope you had a really good Christmas and Joe is doing well. It is snowing quite heartily here now. It probably is in the North of England too, and how beautiful it must be."

15th January 1993

"My sister has only just gone back to the States. It has been wonderful to have her here for so long. We will miss her and her daughter Melissa a lot. However, we are going to do 'Fallen Angels' in Australia next March for 12 weeks, and we are both thrilled. I am really happy to be going back there. I love the country and the people."

21st April 1994

"Hope all is well with you and your splendid boy Joe. I shall be touring in the Autumn in a musical play called 'The Card'. Maybe we will be coming somewhere near your neck of the woods. It would be so nice to see you again."

25th April 1995

(on hearing of my Mother's passing)

"I was so sad and sorry to hear your Mother's had passed on, really a loss that can never be replaced in your life. How lucky you were able to be with her - as we progress through life it seems we reverse the role and end up looking after parents as they love and nurtured us - if we're lucky and your dear Mum obviously was one of the lucky ones. As you said, she was very loving and her love is alive in you and in Joe. You both carry her and each other in your hearts. Surely the greatest thing a parent does, is to teach it's offspring how to love, and love being the greatest power on earth for good, is God manifest. Hate and anger are temporary, whereas love lasts forever. My thoughts go with you Love Hayley x"

8th August 1995

"We have started rehearsals at the Kings Head with the wonderful Julie Covington. The play is emotional, complex, and a challenge in a small space."

23rd October 1995

"My boys are doing well. Ace has just returned from 6 weeks travelling around India with friends, and has greatly benefited from the experience. He has grown up a lot, and is quite content within himself. Crispian has just signed a really good deal with Columbia Records, and now he, and his band 'Kula Shaker', are on the road… If you are up in

London before next January, come and see 'Dead Guilty' at the Apollo."

2nd January 1996

"In the meantime, keep your eyes peeled for Crispian's band Kula Shaker. Their first single came out late last year and has sold well. They will be embarking on an album within the next few months."

10th January 1999

"You must be so proud of Joe, 11 GCSE's and a double 'A' in science. Wow, that's impressive! Please congratulate him from me. He is such a clever chap. You have been a very good dad, I know, and I'm sure he is a well adjusted young man, happy and loved."

28th April 1999

"I have been travelling over the last 12 months mostly in America, and after finishing 'The King and I' somehow could not stop living out of a suitcase… A little bird told me that you have since become a movie star! Congratulations, I look forward to your debut."

(A reference to the making of 'Oliver Twist' in Alston, 1999, I was the bartender in the background of one scene, so don't blink!)

10th June 1999

"Thank you for sending the Noel Coward album. It looks amazing - next time I go to my dad's, I will take it. I know he will love it. Thank you, it was so sweet of you indeed, to think about him."

5th January 2001

"We had a lovely time, and W.H.Y was sent off in great style. We will all be sad when we walked out of the door for the last time, but change is good, inevitable and exciting."

8th May 2002

"It is a stimulating and vibrant city where I have developed a great affection and admiration for New York."

21st April 2003

"The blossom is coming out all over New York. Suddenly, this grey stone and concrete city is transposed by the giddy white cherry blossom - the whole character of the city changes and with it, the spirit of the inhabitants."

13th May 2005

"If you are in the vicinity this weekend, do pop in for a cup of tea if you would like to. Hope all is well, love and many thanks again Hayley x"

15th June 2005

(Hayley's tribute to her father)

"He is, of course, still here, and will always be alive and vibrant in me and in us all. So much emotion, so much love, and great pride. We are all very lucky to lose someone we love, and yet still share all that love."

24th April 2007

(Hayley on celebrating her 61st birthday.)

"And yes, I am 16, I've always been 16, and I will always be 16, somewhere inside!"

18th June 2008

(On the celebration of the birth of my granddaughter)

"Oh! What can I say - you're theirs for life, are they not? So, enjoy this gift that life has bestowed on you - and as they say, when it gets too exhausting, you can hand the little angel right back to mum and dad!"

9th June 2009

"My brother and his wife are visiting from Tasmania, we have not seen them for 4 years. So it was an unusual experience for the three of us to be together again. Last Sunday, we all went to Richmond and took photos of each other outside 'The Wick' on Richmond Hill...... I was touched by you being at Juliet's 1961 wedding at Cowden. I had forgotten we go back that far!"

28th December 2010

"I do wish you the best in everything for the New Year.

PS, I hope I'm in London next time you are down."

27th June 2012

"Dear Trevor, good to hear from you. Glad to know you're able to see the show in Cambridge. Do come round to the stage door afterwards and have a glass of wine in my dressing room. Look forward to seeing you, Love Hayley x" (email)

23rd April 2014

"I hope you had a good Easter, despite the inclement weather. And I hope all is well with you, Joe and his family. Thank you again, dear Trevor."

26th April 2015

"Leave on Tuesday for Australia for 5 months, to start rehearsing for a play with Juliet called 'Legend'. I think we will have fun. It's a funny play with two really good parts for both of us. Two old actresses who have seen better days and can't stand the sight of each other! Luckily, we get on well!"

13th December 2015

"I do hope you can get to Richmond to see the show. As pantos go, it is one of the best! I am really enjoying myself. It's like being a child again. I'm the fairy Godmother who keeps popping on and off, but as long as I can remember which are my cues - I'm fine!"

6th January 2017

"When you are next down in London, let me know, and let's try to make that photograph happen!" (alluding to the fact despite all the years of contact, we have never had a photograph together!)

26th April 2018

"Many, many thanks for the enchanting box of daffodils that you sent for my birthday - they lasted a long time and were a reminder of how lucky I was to be born in the Spring!"

3rd September 2019

"All is well, apart from the normal ills of the flesh being heir to'getting old is not for sissies', the words of the immortal Bette Davis. And I am far too busy with grandchildren, and life in general for work! Having said that, I have started to put down a few thoughts for my memoirs. It seems a good move, while I can still remember my name!"

2nd October 2019

(The reply to my email observation of whether there was the possibility of an autobiography on the way?)

"Dear Trevor,

You're very prescient. Motivator Crispian is driving me!"

8th September 2021

"Dear Trevor, here it is 'Forever Young'. I hope you enjoy it.

Much love,

Hayley x"

8th October 2022

(Accompanied by a family friend, I met up with Hayley after her matinee performance of 'The Best Exotic Marigold Hotel' in Newcastle-Upon-Tyne)

"Dear Trevor,

It was a full moon last night, so the high fells must have looked incredibly beautiful, bathed in its light as you drove home. It was good to see you again after so long, and I liked Victoria enormously. You obviously lead a rich life in the North Pennines and blessed with many friends. Take care of yourself, and please, next time you speak to Joe, will you say Hello and give him my love?

Much Love to You,

Hayley x."

27th February 2023.

"Thank you so much, dear Trevor, for remembering my last night with the Marigold Hotel. How sweet of you. It was very emotional, but we had two of the best shows as a result in dear old Birmingham. I will definitely miss the show and the wonderful Company."

Reading these various comments had a profound effect on me. Our friendship has been quite a remarkable journey. It started as a teenage infatuation, which evolved into a lasting friendship. The pivotal point was that first encounter, where, like a book, it was the content, rather than the cover, that made such a lasting impression.

EPILOGUE

Hayley said to me on one occasion, age is but a number, which is true. For me, it indicates the number of times you have travelled around the Sun! That puts history into perspective! Since the French invaded us in 1066, our planet had gone round the Sun in just under a thousand times! What I find ageless, is the human spirit. Yes, of course, the house where the spirit resides grows old. Bit like an old country cottage, where the thatch wears thin, the plumbing gets a tad suspect, and let's not even mention the foundations! The spirit, that positive energy that makes you the person you are, never appears to change. Perhaps it is this that helps us appreciate all the positive and beautiful aspects of living on planet Earth, and also helps us overcome the negative areas of life.

Sometimes, I pull out the collection of letters received from Hayley over the years and have a quiet browse. It is always a time to reflect on our very different but connected life paths through the decades. We still keep in touch, usually by email now. Among the collection are a letter or two from Crispian and Jason and Sir John. All this from a chance meeting in 1963, with Hayley hanging over a gate on her parents' farm in Kent! Amazing, but then life can be amazing. Fame never tapped me on the shoulder, but life has been full of wonderful events. Yes, of course, we all experience ups and downs in life, but I believe you need to have a few duff moments to really value the 'up' moments! I believe Hayley shares the same view. She still keeps busy with drama, writing and television, where I have also found joy in writing, plus continuing with music. That's the point, it is so important to keep active, both physically and mentally, just to keep the grey matter from seizing up!

Both Hayley and myself enjoy spending as much time as possible with our respective families, especially the grandchildren. It is so easy to keep in contact with modern technology from the comfort of your home, unlike back in the fifties and sixties, where I can remember frequently, standing in freezing street corner telephone boxes, fumbling through pockets for enough penny pieces to pay for the call!

Interestingly, many years ago, while waiting in the Yvonne Arnaud theatre, where Hayley was performing in The Secretary Bird, I found a quiet corner, and amused myself, by not only indulging in my favourite pastime of enjoying a mug of latte, but also studying the gathering throng of people flooding into the theatre. The realisation swept over me, we are all walking stories. Every person has a life story to tell. This was mine.

It's been a joy, and a privilege, to share these stories of Hayley and myself by recounting how our two lives kept in touch for six decades. Of course, the final curtain call must go to you, dear reader.

LETTERS

Now more than ever before has the veil of mystery been lifted on celebrity culture. For a longtime the limelight of the movie and music industries shrouded our pop-idols and movie stars, often creating a hysteria around them that made those lucky enough to 'make it big' seem almost Godly to the rest of us.

The commonly known truth, thanks to social media and reality TV, is that those undoubtedly talented people are no different from the rest of us. These days it may come as no revelation that they have the same frailties, flaws, hopes and desires.

My friendship with Hayley has been based not on her fame, because if it had, the friendship would not have lasted. It would have been very one-sided in my favour. Rather, it was based on two people who found that one another's lives, stories and characters resonated with the other's, which is surely a sound basis for any lasting friendship.

Perhaps the only element of a good friendship that has not been readily available in ours is shared experience. This book illustrates the point because it tells of how our two paths wove their way in completely different directions, crossing only occasionally, usually in a theatre dressing room or nearby tea-room… or by way of letter.

I have received no less than one hundred and eighty letters and postcards from Hayley over the years and have written just as many in return.

These are a selection of those I have received.

White Horse Yard, 1992:

Letter from Hayley to Trevor 8th August, c.1980:

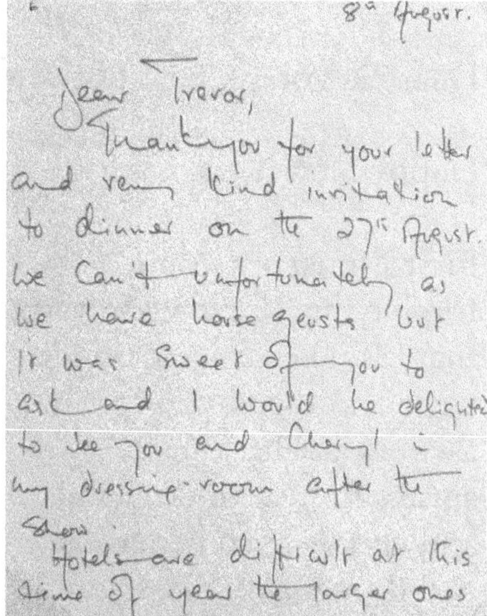

Dear Trevor,

Thankyou for your letter and very kind invitation to dinner on the 27th August. We can't unfortunately as we have house guests but it was sweet of you to ask and I would be delighted to see you and Cheryl in my dressing room after the show.
Hotels are difficult at this time of year as the larger ones are your best bet, "The Dolphin and Anchor" and "The Ship". They get very booked up so its wise to book immediately.

All the best to you both and love,
Hayley

Letter from Hayley to Trevor, Jan 1999:

Dear Trevor,

Happy New Year!

First I must ask you to forgive me, I'm terribly sorry that it's taken me so long to write and thank you for the flowers at Christmas. As always they were beautiful and you were so generous and thoughtful. Bless you. I hope you had a very happy time yourself.

Did you see Joe? You must be so proud of him – 11 GCSE's and double A in science. Wow! That's impressive. Please congratulate him for me. He's a clever chap. I'm sure you must miss him. You've been a very good Dad I know, and I'm sure he's a well adjusted young man, happy and loved – which is one of the reasons he did so well at school. From the moment they are born our objective is to help our children to leave us. To go out into the world, its agony sometime isn't it , but that's what its all about I guess.

I know I haven't responded to your request about doing something for your local school – the thing is, well, I've been in America a lot and also I really haven't got any idea what I could do, I mean that would be interesting and worthwhile folks making the effort to leave their cozy hearths and homes! But, I will as you say, "give it some thought" – now I'm home for a few weeks! Life has been unsettled to say the least. "The King and I" knocked me sideways and it's taken months literally to recover, actually I don't think I'll ever be quite the same again – maybe that's a good thing!
I hope you are well and happy. Give my love to Jenny & much love to you.
Hayley

Letter from Hayley to Trevor, June 2005

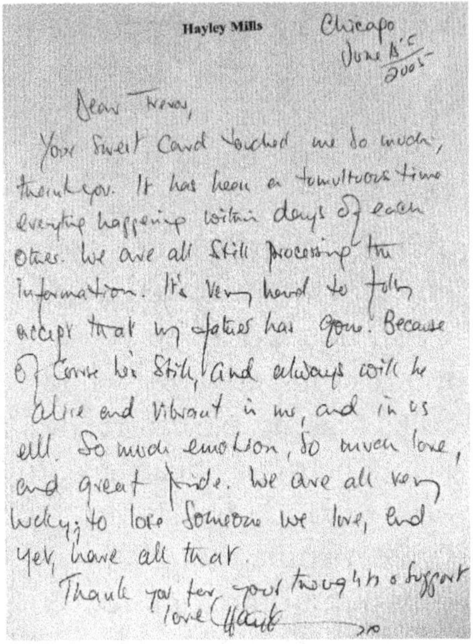

Hayley Mills

Chicago
June [illegible]
2005

Dear Trevor,

Your sweet card touched me so much, thank you. It has been a tumultuous time everything happening within days of each other. We are all still processing the information. It's very hard to fully accept that my father has gone. Because of course he's still, and always will be alive and vibrant in me, and in us all. So much emotion, so much love, and great pride. We are all very lucky; to lose someone we love, and yet, have all that.

Thank you for your thoughts & support

love [illegible]

Dear Trevor,

Your sweet card touched me so much, thank you. It has been a tumultuous time everything happening within days of each other. We are all still processing the information. It's very hard to truly accept that my father has gone. Because of course he's still, and always will be alive and vibrant in me, and in us all. So much emotion, so much love, and great friend. We are all very lucky. To lose someone we love, and yet, have all that.

Thank you for your thought and support.

Love, Hayley

Letter from Hayley to Trevor, 4th January 2014

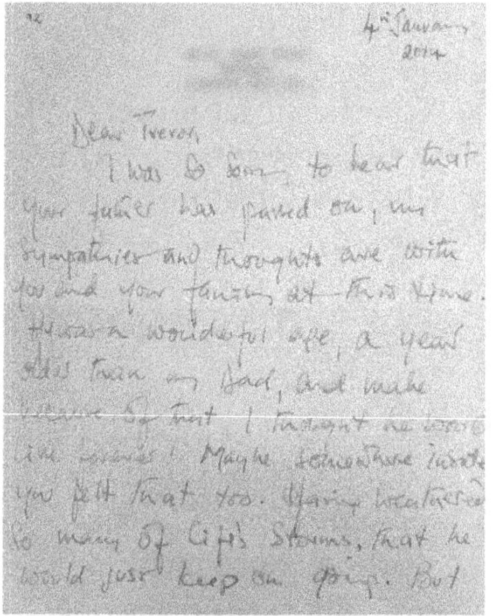

Dear Trevor,

I was so sorry to hear that your father has passed on, my sympathies and thoughts are with you and your family at this time.

He was a wonderful age, a year older than my Dad, and maybe because of that I thought he would live forever! Maybe somewhere inside you felt that too. Having weathered so many of life's storms that he would just keep on going. But how wonderful for him, and for all of you that he died so quickly, so peacefully. Just like my Dad. It's a great gift to those he's left behind.
But the void will always be there, the world that was him, and you and all that life and all those memories – are now just that, just memories. And gratitude. Memories and gratitude and love.
Thinking of you.
With love,
Hayley

Letter from Hayley to Trevor, date unknown

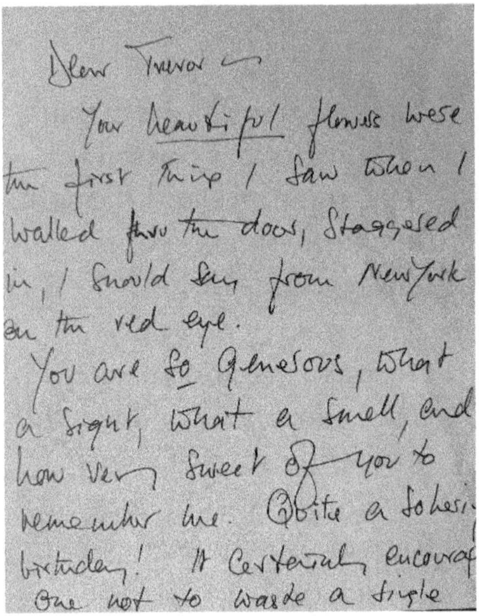

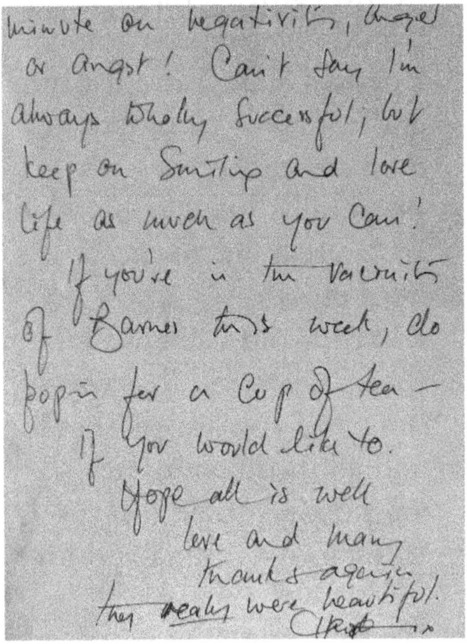

Dear Trevor,

Your beautiful flowers were the first thing I saw when I walked through the doors, staggered in, I should say from New York on the red eye. You are so generous, what a sight, what a smell, and how very sweet of you to remember me. Quite a <soheriy birthday! It certainly encourages one not to waste a single minute on negativities, anger or angst. Can't say I'm always wholly successful, but keep on smiling and love life as much as you can!
If you're in the vicinity of Barnes this week, do pop in for a cup of tea – if you would like to.
Hope all is well.

Love and many thoughts again. They really were beautiful.
Hayley x

ABOUT THE AUTHOR

Trevor Wright was born in 1945, during the midst of WWII. Family created a rich environment for a young imagination to thrive and so it comes as no surprise that there are many stories of hard, fastidious work as reflected by his mother and father and the adventuresome antics of his elder sisters. Trevor learned at a young age that life is what you make of it and he has continued on that vein ever since. Writing is not a lifelong career for him, but a passion on a long list of passions that includes (and is not limited to) founder of a startup accident repair garage, a commercial haulage firm, and then owner of a riding stables. He has been a musician, an actor, a playwright and an author (not just of this book). It is this zest for life and his unyielding enthusiasm for adventure that makes his half of this story so compelling. His six-decade friendship with the celebrity Hayley Mills is testament to his outlook on life, his honest and grounded 'what-you-see-is-what-you-get' demeanor and his belief in the human spirit. Unlike many people that are not in the world of celebrity, but do have the opportunity to get to know them, he always thought of Hayley as a friend, rather than an object of affection as is so common for people who share her world.

www.ingramcontent.com/pod-product-compliance
Lightning Source LLC
LaVergne TN
LVHW012049160826
845678LV00014B/2761

* 9 7 8 0 9 5 6 3 9 4 8 2 8 *